Media Law in South Korea

Media Law in South Korea

Ahran Park
Minjeong Kim
Yoonmo Sang

This book was originally published as a monograph in the International Encyclopaedia of Laws/Media Law.

Founding Editor: Roger Blanpain
General Editor: Frank Hendrickx
Volume Editors: Peggy Valcke & Eva Lievens

Wolters Kluwer

Published by:
Kluwer Law International B.V.
PO Box 316
2400 AH Alphen aan den Rijn
The Netherlands
E-mail: international-sales@wolterskluwer.com
Website: lrus.wolterskluwer.com

Sold and distributed by:
Wolters Kluwer Legal & Regulatory U.S.
7201 McKinney Circle
Frederick, MD 21704
United States of America
E-mail: customer.service@wolterskluwer.com

ISBN 978-94-035-3984-3

e-Book: ISBN 978-94-035-3985-0
web-PDF: ISBN 978-94-035-3991-1

The Authors*

Ahran Park is a Principal Researcher of the Media Research Center of the Korea Press Foundation in Seoul, South Korea. Her main research interests are in media law and policy, on which she has published extensively, especially in relation to Internet law and regulation. She completed her M.A. from Seoul National University and Ph.D. from the School of Journalism and Communication at the University of Oregon, U.S.A. She was a former news reporter of *Chosun Daily* Newspaper in Seoul. She has frequently acted as an expert advisor to the Ministry of Culture, Sports and Tourism in South Korea. She published Korean media law books and articles in Korean and international journals. She also contributed to comparative media law books such as *Justices and Journalists: The Global Perspective*, *International Libel and Privacy Handbook*, and *Carter-Ruck on Libel and Privacy*.

Minjeong Kim is Professor of Media and Communication at the Hankuk University of Foreign Studies in Seoul, South Korea. Minjeong's areas of expertise include communication law and policy, copyright law, and digital media. Her research has been published in scholarly journals including *Communication Law and Policy, Journal of Copyright Society of USA, Journal of Computer-Mediated Communication*, and *Telecommunications Policy*. She completed her M.A. and Ph.D. from the School of Journalism and Mass Communication at the University of North Carolina at Chapel Hill. Before joining the HUFS faculty in fall 2013, Minjeong was an associate professor at Colorado State University in Fort Collins, CO, U.S.A. and an assistant professor at Hawaii Pacific University in Honolulu, HI, U.S.A.

*. This study was financially supported in part by the Institute of Communication Research, Seoul National University.

The Authors

Yoonmo Sang (Ph.D., The University of Texas at Austin) is Assistant Professor in the Department of Media & Communication at Sungshin Women's University (effective September 1, 2021). He was formerly Senior Lecturer at the University of Canberra and Assistant Professor at Howard University. His primary research interests center on the intersection of new media technologies and the law, focusing on how socio-cultural and technological changes advantage and/or disadvantage different stakeholders. He is on the editorial boards of four journals: *Digital Journalism*, *Social Media + Society*, *Communication Law Review*, and the *Journal of Media Law, Ethics, and Policy Research*, a journal of the Korean Society for Media Law, Ethics, and Policy Research.

Table of Contents

List of Abbreviations

CBS	Christian Broadcasting System
CJB	Cheongju Broadcasting
DMB	Digital Multimedia Broadcasting
DMZ	Demilitarized Zone
DPRK	Democratic People's Republic of Korea
EBS	Educational Broadcasting System
FBC	Foundation for Broadcast Culture
G1	Gangwon No. 1 Broadcasting
IPTV	Internet Protocol Television
ISP	Internet Service Provider
JIBS	Jeju Free International City Broadcasting System
JTV	Jeonju Television Corporation
KBC	Kwangju Broadcasting Corporation
KBS	Korean Broadcasting System
KCC	Korea Communications Commission
KCSC	Korea Communications Standards Commission
KISS	Koreanstudies Information Service System
KNN	Korea New Network
KOSIS	Korean Statistical Information Service
MBC	Munhwa Broadcasting Corporation
PAC	Press Arbitration Commission
RISS	Research Information Sharing Service
ROK	Republic of Korea
SBS	Seoul Broadcasting System
TBC	Taegu Broadcasting Corporation
TBS	Traffic Broadcasting System
TJB	Taejon Broadcasting Corporation
UBC	Ulsan Broadcasting Corporation

List of Abbreviations

General Introduction

§1. GENERAL BACKGROUND OF THE COUNTRY

I. Political and Legal System of the Country

1. South Korea, officially the Republic of Korea (ROK), is a democratic republic. After the Japanese Occupation (1905–1945) and the surrender of Japan in 1945 at the end of the Pacific War, the 38th parallel line divided Korea when the United States and the Soviet Union stepped into the Korean Peninsula. After the Korean War (1950–1953), the Republic of Korea (ROK) was set up in the southern half of the Korean Peninsula while a communist government, the Democratic People's Republic of Korea (DPRK), was installed in the north. Currently, the peninsula is split along a Demilitarized Zone (DMZ) at the 38th parallel.

2. The Constitution of 1987 proclaims Korea to be a democratic republic, with three branches: Executive, Legislature, and the Judiciary. No laws may violate constitutional principles. Laws are enacted by the National Assembly, the legislative branch of the Korean government. The executive branch has the authority to issue rules and regulations, as well as to submit bills to the National Assembly. The Constitution empowers the president to issue emergency orders in the face of internal turmoil, external menace, natural calamity, or a grave financial or economic crisis.

3. The National Assembly, the Supreme Court, and the Constitutional Court have the authority to adopt regulations relating to judicial proceedings and internal rules for the conduct of court business. The Constitution provides for legislative procedures during times of national emergency.

4. South Korea has an ordinary court system and a Constitutional Court. There are six types of ordinary courts in Korea, which are the Supreme Court, the High Courts, the District Courts, the Patent Court, the Family Court, and the Administrative Court. The District Courts (courts of original jurisdiction that include a family court and an administrative court), the High Courts (intermediate appellate courts) and the Supreme Court (the highest judicial tribunal) are the courts for the basic three-tier system. The Patent Court is on the same level as the High Courts, and the Family Court and the Administrative court are on the same level as the District Courts.

5. The Supreme Court, which comprises a chief justice and thirteen other justices, makes rulings via the grand bench (*en banc*) or a petty bench.[1] The grand bench gathers with more than two-thirds of the justices and enters judgments by simple majority. The court also has three petty benches, each convened with four justices. The court is authorized to review the constitutionality of administrative rules and regulations, but not statutes.

6. Apart from the general courts, Korea has the European-type Constitutional Court, which adjudicates on the constitutionality of laws, impeachment, the dissolution of political parties, competence dispute, and constitutional complaint.[2] A judicial review decision by the Constitutionals Court cannot be appealed, binding all state agencies and local governments.

7. The Constitutional Court is made up of nine justices appointed by the president, with the consent of the National Assembly, for a six-year term. The proceedings at the court are conducted through a full bench, not as a panel. A full bench requires the attendance of seven or more justices. Since the Constitutional Court was established in 1988, the Constitutional Court has contributed to consolidating democracy and protecting human rights in South Korea.

II. Geography and Population

8. South Korea is located in the southern part of the Korean Peninsula. To the west is the People's Republic of China, with the West Sea in between. In the east, Japan is across the East Sea. The capital is Seoul and the flag is *Taekeukgi*.

9. The current population of South Korea as of January 2021 is 51,821,699, based on the latest Korean Statistical Information Service (KOSIS) estimates. South Korea ranks number twenty-eight in the list of countries by population.

III. Social and Cultural Values

10. Korea was supposed to become a participatory constitutional polity. However, it was not until the mid-1980s that Korea emerged into a rule-of-law democracy out of its perennial rule-by-law authoritarianism. The Korean media are free and they do not worry about the kind of external constraints that they had to cope with prior to 1987.

1. Supreme Court of Korea, http://eng.scourt.go.kr/eng/main/Main.work.
2. Constitutional Court of Korea, http://english.ccourt.go.kr/cckhome/eng/index.do.

§2. The Media Landscape

I. Overview of Media Markets and Main Actors

11. South Korea, a media-rich nation, has numerous cable, terrestrial, and satellite television stations and more than five-hundred daily newspapers in Korean and English. Although broadcasting industry is often subject to governmental influence, political and economic liberalization has helped news media industry thriving.

12. South Korea has a unique registration system for newspapers, Internet newspapers, magazines, and other periodicals. Under the Act of Promotion of Newspapers, a person who intends to publish a newspaper, an online newspaper, or online news service shall have the name of the newspaper, type and frequency of publication, the publisher's name and address etc. registered with the Mayor or other governors. Article 12 of the Act of Promotion of Newspapers states that the Mayor or governor should submit matters of newspaper registration or the closure of newspaper business to the Minister of Culture, Sports and Tourism on a quarterly basis. A person who intends to publish a magazine must also register the required matters to the Mayor or other governors under the Act on Promotion of Periodicals, which is very similar to the Act of Promotion of Newspapers.

13. As of December 2020, the number of registered periodicals was 22,837 in total: 328 daily newspapers, 1,188 weekly newspapers, 9,584 Internet newspapers, 5,492 magazines, and other periodicals. According to the Korea Press Foundation's 2020 Audience Research Report, printed newspapers continued to lose their ground in readership and subscription. The newspaper readership rate stood at 10.2% in 2020, compared with the 1996 readership rate of 85.2%. The print newspaper subscription rate was 9.5% in 2018, down from 9.9% a year earlier.

II. Broadcasting Infrastructure

14. As of December 2019, there are thirty terrestrial TV, thirty-one relay cables, ninety-two cable system operators, thirty-six IPTV (Internet Protocol Television) content providers, twenty-one terrestrial radios, and nineteen terrestrial DMB (Digital Multimedia Broadcasting). The four major broadcasting networks are KBS (Korean Broadcasting System), MBC (Munhwa Broadcasting Corporation), SBS (Seoul Broadcasting System), and EBS (Educational Broadcasting System).

III. Technological and Economic Developments on the Media Markets

15. Korea has the best Internet connectivity in the world. The Internet has become an essential part in Koreans' life. Nearly 91.8% of citizens are using the Internet, and 99.7% of households have access to a computer and a mobile Internet connection.[3] As the number of smartphone users has increased, digital platforms have become the dominant means to access online contents.

§3. Sources of Media Law

16. Media law is a substantial area of free speech jurisprudence in Korea. The Constitution guarantees freedom of speech and the press in Article 21(1), which provides, "All citizens shall enjoy freedom of speech, press, assembly, and association."[4]

17. The Constitution, however, limits the freedom of the press with Article 21(4), stating that freedom of the press must not violate the rights of individuals, and compensation for damage should be made if the press infringes an individual's right. If the press infringes on other people's rights, damage should be compensated.[5] The Constitution regulates the freedom of the press without giving any preferred positions to the press compared with other human rights.

18. Primary sources of law are written laws. Written laws have four main categories: (1) statutes passed by the legislature; (2) decrees issued by the President, cabinet, ministries, the Supreme Court, and the Constitutional Court; (3) rules and regulations by government agencies, local government, and international agreements; (4) treaties as rules of international law with same effect as the domestic laws.

19. Secondary sources of law are court's decisions, law reviews, journals, scholarly articles, and legal news. Although there is no principle of *stare decisis*, Article 8 of the Court Organization Act states: "Any decision made in a judgment of a higher court shall bind the court of lower instance with respect to the case in question." The websitc of the Supreme Court and the Constitutional Court provide selected court's decisions translated into English. LAWnB,[6] the most comprehensive legal database in Korea, provides statutes, court decisions, law reviews, scholarly articles, and legal news. The websites of the National Library[7] and the National Assembly Library[8] also have a database on all topics, including law. The most popular general scholarly databases are DBpia,[9] KISS (Koreanstudies Information Service System),[10] and RISS (Research Information Sharing Service).[11]

3. Ministry of Science, ICT and Future Planning, annual report (2019).
4. Constitution of the Republic of Korea Art. 21(1) (1987).
5. Article 21(4) of the Constitution states: "Neither speech nor the press shall violate the honor nor the rights of other persons not undermine public morals or social ethics. Should speech or the press violate the honor or rights of the persons, claims may be made for damage resulting therefrom."
6. LAWnB, https://www.lawnb.com.
7. National Library of Korea, https://www.nl.go.kr/EN/main/index.do.
8. National Assembly Library, https://www.nanet.go.kr/main.do.
9. DBPIA, http://m.dbpia.co.kr.
10. KISS, http://kiss.kstudy.com.
11. RISS, http://www.riss.kr/index.do.

Lawtimes,[12] one of the daily legal newspapers, supplies legal news, court decisions, and legal information.

12. Lawtimes, https://www.lawtimes.co.kr.

Part I. Freedom of Speech

20. The Constitution strongly protects the freedom of speech and the press. Article 21(1) says: "all citizens shall enjoy freedom of speech and the press, and freedom of assembly and association." Article 21(2) states that licencing or censorship of speech and the press shall not be recognized.

21. Freedom of speech and the press, however, is not absolute. The Constitution limits freedom of speech and the press, emphasizing that it should not violate the honor or rights of other persons or undermine public morals or social ethics under Article 21(4).

22. Article 3 of the Act on Press Arbitration and Remedies, etc. for Damage Caused by Press Reports (hereinafter referred to as "Press Arbitration Act") also protects freedom and independence of the press. Article 3 declares:

(1) The freedom and independence of the press shall be guaranteed.
(2) No person shall regulate on or interfere with the freedom and independence of the press.
(3) The press shall have rights to have free access to information sources, and freedom to publish covered information.
(4) Freedom and rights referred to in paragraphs 1 through 3 shall not be restricted, except as otherwise provided by the Constitution and Acts.

23. Censorship of expression or prior restraint is prohibited by the Constitution. South Korea had a provision that prohibits censorship in the Constitution of the Third Republic, but it has been removed in the Constitution of the Fourth and Fifth Republics. The current Constitution restored it under Article 21(2). The Constitutional Court, relying on Article 21(2), ruled that a prior restraint requires all of the following four elements: (1) an obligation to submit an expression for permission, (2) a pre-examination procedure that is subject to an administrative authority, (3) prohibition of expressions without permission, (4) a compulsory means to carry out the examination process.[13]

24. Freedom of speech on the Internet is strongly protected under the Constitution. One of the major decisions related to online speech is the "Online Verification System" case in 2012. The Act on Promotion of Information and Communications

13. Constitutional Court, decided on August 30, 2001, 2000Hunga9.

Network Utilization and Information Protection Act (hereinafter referred to as "Information and Communications Network Act") regulated Internet Service Providers (ISPs) by imposing duties of confirming online user's identity and maintaining user's identity information through a verification process. The Constitutional Court ruled that the identity verification scheme had a chilling effect on people's expression of opinion and restricted freedom of expression guaranteed by the Constitution, amounting to an obstacle for free public opinions and democratic society. Thus, the provision was ruled as unconstitutional because it violated freedom of expression and the right of self-determination on private information.

25. Likewise, Article 82(6) of the Public Official Election Act stipulates that Internet media companies should check their users' names when the users post comments on political parties or candidates on bulletin boards and chat rooms during the election campaign period. On January 28, 2021, the Constitutional Court ruled that such regulation was unconstitutional on the ground that it prohibited freedom of anonymous speech and the right of personal information regarding political expression.[14]

26. There was another important case related to freedom of online expression. In 2008, Dae-sung Park, who was a famous online guru with his username "Minerva," posted articles on a popular Korean online portal site, "Daum." Criticizing the government's economic policy, Park argued that the currency exchange was halted because the Korean foreign reserve was drained. His postings caused a panic among online users and made stock prices drop.

27. Park was charged for the violation of Article 47(1) of the Electric Telecommunication Act, which penalizes anybody "who has publicly made a false communication through the electric telecommunication facilities and equipment with the intent to harm the public interest" by imprisonment for no more than five years or by a fine not exceeding KRW 50 million.[15] Park filed a motion to request for the review of constitutionality of the law at issue.

28. On December 28, 2010, the Constitutional Court declared Article 47(1) of the Electric Telecommunication Act unconstitutional. According to the court, Article 47(1) was subject to the rule of clarity on a strict level because the provision was a restrictive legislation on freedom of expression with criminal penalties:

> The "public interest" used here is such unclear and abstract that it seems to be the rewriting of the constitutional provisions which prescribes minimum conditions to restrict basic rights and the limitation of the constitutional freedom of speech and the press. Whether a certain expression violates the public interest drastically varies depending on individual's value system and ethical standard. This is also true even when legal professionals interpret the meaning of

---

14. Constitutional Court, decided on January 28, 2021, 2018Hunma456.
15. The South Korean *won* is the official currency of South Korea. As of February 9, 2021, USD 1 of the current exchange rates is 1,116 *won*.

> the public interest. Further, its meaning cannot be fixed by the legal professionals' customary work of interpretation of law … . The law does not notify ordinary citizens of what purpose of communication is prohibited. It is unconstitutional by violating the rule of clarity applied to the freedom of expression.[16]

29. Although Article 47(1) of the Electric Telecommunication Act was rescinded, Article 47(2) of the Act is still effective. Article 47(2) penalizes a person who publicizes a false communication on the Internet for the purpose of benefiting himself or inflicting damages on a third party.

16. Constitutional Court, decided on December 28, 2010, 2008Hun-Ba157; 2009Hun-Ba88 (consolidated).

Part II. Regulation of Print Media

Chapter 1. The Journalists' Profession

30. The basic code that applies to journalists is the Charter of the Press Ethics, which was enacted by the Journalists Association of Korea and the Korea Internet Newspaper Association.[17] The Charter of the Press Ethics proclaims that the press should be ethical and responsible for the public's right to know. The Journalists Association of Korea has its own Code of Conducts for Journalists, which provides guidelines for news report related to human rights, sexual crime, suicide and disaster.[18]

31. Generally, bloggers are not considered journalists. For instance, bloggers are not allowed to get into the press room located in the courts and public prosecutors' offices, for only the journalists affiliated with major news companies are permitted to enter and utilize the official press rooms.[19] Law does not provide any special protections for blogger journalists as well. Nonetheless, bloggers often have played important roles in revealing political issues regarding public interests. OhmyNews, founded in 2000, is the most famous online news website that publishes citizen reporter.

32. The Press Arbitration Act aims to make freedom of the press compatible with public responsibilities by establishing an effective remedial system.[20] Article 2 of the Act defines the press as "any broadcasting, newspaper, periodical including any magazine, news agency or online newspaper."

17. Journalists Association of Korea & the Korea Internet Newspaper Association, Charter of the Press Ethics, http://www.journalist.or.kr/news/section4.html?p_num=18.
18. Journalists Association of Korea, Code of Conduct for Journalists, http://www.journalist.or.kr/news/section4.html?p_num=1.
19. Seung-hyun Kim, *Pressroom, Our Twisted Workplace*, 126 Kwan-hun Journal 235 (2013).
20. Press Arbitration Act, Art. 1.

Chapter 2. Journalists' Rights

§1. Role of Journalists as Watchdogs of Society

33. The Korean Constitutional Court has recognized the importance of journalist's role as watchdog: "The public's right to know depends on news media, which enables the public to actively discuss social issues and politics. The press that works as a watchdog and reflects public opinion is quite substantial for our democracy. In this context, the marketplace of ideas and the role of the press are quintessential in democracy."[21]

34. The watchdog function of the media was sometimes rejected in the past. Under the military rule until the mid-1980s, some Korean commentators argued that major Korean newspapers and broadcasting stations acted as "lapdogs" of the military rulers. Since 1987, however, Korean news media have undergone the remarkable change from an authoritarian press to a libertarian system.

§2. Journalists' Independence

35. Article 3 of the Press Arbitration Act declares that freedom and independence of the press shall be guaranteed: "no person shall regulate on or interfere with the freedom and independence of the press." Article 3(4) emphasizes that freedom and rights of the press shall be restricted only by the Constitution and other acts.

36. Article 4 of the Press Arbitration Act states:

(1) Press report shall be impartial and objective and ensure the protection and expansion of citizens' rights to know and their freedom of speech.
(2) The press shall respect human dignity and shall neither defame others nor infringe on their rights, public morals and social ethics.
(3) The press shall advocate the public interest in the public concern and perform its public duties for the purpose of contributing to the formation of democratic public opinions by news gathering, reporting, comments or other means.

§3. Protection of Journalistic Sources

I. Statutory Law

37. The Press Basic law, which was enacted in 1980, permitted journalists to refuse to reveal private information of news source under Article 8. After the Press

21. Constitutional Court, decided on June 24, 1999, 97 Hunma 265.

Basic Law was abolished in 1987, there is no general statutory protection for journalists in South Korea. Courts have not ruled on journalist's privilege due to the absence of statutory protection for journalist.

38. Under the Criminal Procedure Act and the Civil Procedure Act, all the citizens are obligated to testify in the courtroom.[22] A witness who does not obey a summons without good cause may be taken into custody.[23] A practicing lawyer, patent attorney, accountant, doctor, dentist, pharmacists, nurse, or a religious functionary may resist seizure of materials in his possession related to other's secret.[24] However, this article does not apply to journalists, so journalists cannot resist seizure of materials in their possession.

39. When a journalist refuses to appear as a witness, the court may order the journalist to pay the litigation expense incurred by his/her non-appearance and may also impose an administrative fine not exceeding KRW 5 million.[25]

40. There is no right for journalists to reject a police request of searching a newsroom. A court may seize any materials connected with the accused case.[26] Hence, journalists must obey the law when a police officer arrives at the newsroom with a valid search and seizure warrant.

II. Whistleblowing

41. Whistleblowers are given protection under the Protection of Public Interest Reporters Act, which was enacted in 2011. The Act was proposed to protect those who have reported any conduct that is detrimental to the public interest.[27]

42. The term "conduct detrimental to the public interest" means certain types of conducts harmful to health and safety of the people, environment, interests of consumers and fair competition.[28]

43. According to Article 15, no person shall take disadvantageous measures against a public interest reporter or no person shall interfere with filling or canceling a public interest report. The whistleblower who got disadvantage may request the Compensation Deliberative Committee to take measures for reinstatement or other necessary measures.[29]

---

22. Criminal Procedure Act, Art. 136; Civil Procedure Act, Art. 303.
23. Criminal Procedure Act, Art. 152.
24. *Ibid.*, Art. 12.
25. *Ibid.*, Art. 151(1).
26. *Ibid.*, Art. 106.
27. Protection of Public Interest Reporters Act, Art. 1.
28. *Ibid.*, Art. 2.
29. *Ibid.*, Art. 17.

Chapter 3. Journalists' Liability

44. The following provisions apply to both print and broadcast journalists. Article 5(1) of the Press Arbitration Act declares:

> The press, any Internet news service, or any Internet multimedia broadcasting shall not infringe on another persons' life, liberty, body, health, reputation, the secrecy and freedom pertaining to privacy, portrait, name, voice, dialogue, works, personal documents, any other personal worth, etc. and, where the press, etc. has infringed on any other person's personality right, such damage shall be remedied promptly in accordance with the procedure prescribed by this Act.

45. When the press invades other's personal rights, the press shall be liable for such infringement. Nevertheless, there are two exemptions for the press under Article 5(2) of the Press Arbitration Act: (1) where an infringement has been done with consent from the sufferer in question; (2) where the news media had reasonable grounds for believing the story to be true and the story related to a matter of public concern.

§1. General Information on the Liability System

46. Liability may lie under criminal law or civil law.

§2. Special Liability Regime for Journalists

47. There is no special liability regime for journalists. They are treated in the same way as other accused persons or defendants.

§3. Defamation (Libel)

I. Defamation Effect

48. Defamation law has serious chilling effects on the freedom of speech and the press in South Korea, for defamation shall be punished under the Criminal Act and compensated under the Civil Act. Furthermore, the Criminal Act punishes defamation even when defamatory comments deliver true facts. Therefore, truth is the conditional defense against prosecutions for defamation.

49. The Criminal Act punishes defamation related to true facts and has aggravated punishment for defamation related to false facts. Thus, the severity of the punishment of criminal defamation relies on whether the defamatory statement is true or false. Article 307 of the Criminal Act states:

1. A person who defames another by publicly alleging facts shall be punished by penal servitude or imprisonment for not more than two years or by a fine not exceeding five million *won.*
2. A person who defames another by publicly alleging false facts shall be punished by penal servitude or imprisonment for not more than five years, by suspension of civil rights for not more than ten years, or by a fine not exceeding ten million *won.*

If a libelous statement is published by newspaper, magazine, radio and other means with intent to defame other, it will be punished more severely under Article 309.

The Civil Act also protects reputation. The victims of defamation may recover their reputational damage by asking monetary compensation for defamation injury or retractions under Article 751:

(1) A person who has injured the person, liberty or fame of another or has inflicted any mental anguish to another person shall be liable to make compensation for damages arising therefrom.
(2) The court may order the guilty party to discharge the compensation mentioned in paragraph 1 by periodical payments and may order such guilty parties to offer reasonable security in order to insure his performance of such obligations.

50. When defamed by the press, the victim may rely on the Press Arbitration Act, which contains a separate clause for a right of reply, a right of correction, and a right to request further report.[30]

51. Online defamation as a crime is regulated by the Information and Communications Network Act. Article 70 of the Act punishes a person who commits defamation through an information and communications network.

II. Reference to the Claimant (Identification)

52. A plaintiff must prove that the defamation was "of and concerning" the plaintiff. Such identification does not require that the plaintiff was named. The plaintiff can be identified by other information within the defamatory material or by other facts not included in the harmful material.

53. The Supreme Court held that the plaintiff could be identified even when an initial or an acronym of the plaintiff was noted in the defamatory statement.[31]

30. For more information about press arbitration, *see* Part V. Supervision: Media Regulator Chapter 1. Organization §3. Press Arbitration Commissio.
31. Supreme Court, decided on May 10, 2002, 2000Da50213.

54. When the defamatory statement was concerning the group that the plaintiff was affiliated with, the plaintiff can be identified if the group has a low number of members.[32]

III. Publication

55. Publication occurs when defamatory material is disseminated to someone other than the person defamed. Publication occurs regardless of whether defamatory material is distributed in written or spoken form.

56. The Criminal Act does not make any difference between slander and libel. When the media commits defamation, however, the punishment shall be aggravated under Article 309:

(1) A person who commits the crime of Article 307(1), by means of newspaper, magazine, radio, or other publication with intent to defame another, shall be punished by imprisonment or imprisonment without prison labor for not more than three years or by a fine not exceeding KRW 7 million.
(2) A person who commits the crime of Article 307(2), by the method described in paragraph (1), shall be punished by imprisonment for not more than seven years or suspension of qualifications for not more than ten years, or a fine not exceeding KRW 15 million.

IV. Capacity to Sue

57. Both persons and corporations are entitled to sue for defamation.

58. The Criminal Act recognizes defamation of the deceased as a crime: "A person who defames the deceased by publicly alleging false facts shall be punished by penal servitude or imprisonment for not more than two years or fined not more than five million *won*."[33]

59. Government and local authorities are not entitled to sue someone for defamation. The Supreme Court held that government and local authorities must be open to criticism as political and administrative bodies, so they cannot be allowed to sue in defamation.[34] The court reasoned that government and local authorities should be freely criticized by citizens and such criticism would be possible when freedom of expression is protected enough.

32. Supreme Court, decided on May 12, 2006, 2004Da35199.
33. Criminal Act, Art. 308.
34. Supreme Court, decided on December 27, 2016, 2014Do15290.

V. Defenses and Evidential Burden

60. Defamation shall be immunized if the allegedly libelous statement is true and contributes to public interest. Article 310 stipulates: "if the facts alleged under Section 1 of Article 307 are true and solely for the public interest, they shall not be punishable."

61. To be immunized, the truth defense does not require that the allegedly libelous statement is perfectly true. The statement may include an erroneous expression or hyperbolical expression to allow more "breathing space" to freedom of speech and the press.[35]

62. When a speaker believed that his/her statement was true, but it is proved as false later on, the speaker shall be immunized if he/she had a "reasonable belief" in the truth of the statement.

63. The "reasonable belief" standard applies to the press as well. The Supreme Court ruled that the journalist had the "reasonable belief" in reporting when he tried to verify all the facts and contact witnesses in a criminal case.[36] However, when a journalist reported a conviction without further interviewing with related persons, the "reasonable belief" was denied in court.[37] Therefore, the "reasonable belief" standard provides more freedom to speakers and journalists while immunizing a false statement in certain circumstances.

64. The "public interest" standard requires the statement would be beneficial or helpful to certain members of a group, a society, or a nation.

65. The evidential burden is on the defendant. As the courts denied recognizing "actual malice"[38] principle in the United States, the burden of proof is not converted even when the plaintiff is a public figure.

VI. Truth

66. Truth is not an absolute defense for defamation. As Article 307(1) states, a true statement can be punishable if the statement harms another person's reputation.

35. Supreme Court, decided on January 22, 2002, 2000Da37524.
36. Supreme Court, decided on August 23, 1996, 94Do3191.
37. Supreme Court, decided on May 28, 1996, 94Da33828.
38. "Actual malice" (i.e., knowledge of falsity or reckless disregard for the truth) is the legal standard established by the U.S. Supreme Court to determine whether public officials or public figures may recover damages in libel lawsuits against the news media.

VII. Opinion

67. For an allegedly defamatory statement to be actionable, the statement must be one of fact. If a defamatory statement involves only opinion, it cannot be actionable.

68. The difficult question is how to distinguish facts from opinions. In 2000, the Supreme Court ruled that a statement may constitute fact if the statement involves implication of existing facts.[39] Therefore, defamatory statement relating to certain facts cannot be immunized, even if the defendant used expressions such as "according to my opinion" and "in my opinion."

VIII. Privilege

69. Neither the Criminal Code nor the Civil Code provides special protection for statements of "fair comment" or "fair report" on matters of public concern.

IX. Publication on a Matter of Public Interest

70. If the alleged defamatory statement involves a public figure or public interest, courts will allow more protection for freedom of speech and the press. When the freedom of the press and the right of reputation conflict each other, the court applies a different standard of review for a public figure or public issues.

71. In 2002, the Supreme Court made a landmark decision to give more protection to the press in publishing defamatory articles.[40] The court held that the judicial scrutiny should vary, depending on "whether the person who allegedly defamed is a public figure or a private figure, whether the statement is about a matter of public concern or of a purely private concern, whether the statement addresses a matter of public and social importance that citizens should be objectively aware of and thus contribute to the formation of public opinion or public debate."

72. The Constitutional Court also held that different standards should be applied between public figures and private figures:

> Depending on whether the victim of the defamatory statement is a public or a private figure and whether the statement is a matter of public concern or a matter in a purely private area, there should be a difference in constitutional standard of review. Restrictions on defamatory statement against a public figure concerning his/her public activities should be relatively more relaxed. This does not mean that a statement about a public figure or a matter of public concern should enjoy unlimited freedom. An attack against an individual that is

---

39. Supreme Court, decided on July 28, 2000, 99Da6203.
40. Supreme Court, decided on January 22, 2002, 2000Da37524.

> malicious or substantially lacks reasonableness and based on a clearly false statement exceeding the acceptable level of exaggeration in the ordinary sense, may be subject to restriction.[41]

73. The Constitutional Court held that even matters concerning a public official's personal life might fall within the scope of public concern in certain cases. For instance, matters relating to a public official's qualifications, ethics, and integrity would hardly be considered to stay within the sphere of purely private life, the court said. Because these matters can offer information necessary for the public to criticize and evaluate social activities of the public official, they might have relevance to his or her official duties. Consequently, the court said that criticisms on such matters should be allowed and the speaker should not be punished under law of defamation.

74. In 2003, the Supreme Court pointed out that more freedom of the press should be allowed to expressions relating to public figures or the public interest. The court held that if the press did not try "a malicious or considerably improbable attack" to the public figure, such expression should be allowed for the watchdog function.[42]

75. In a case related to MBC, the Supreme Court held that the broadcasting company did not defame Korean cabinet ministers by "a malicious or considerably improbable attack" with the MBC producer's critical comment about governmental negotiation with the U.S. government.[43]

76. When the former Prime Minister Hae-chan Lee sued a regional newspaper for defamation, the Supreme Court found the newspaper reporter to be "malicious" in publishing that the Prime Minister enjoyed a "liquor party" amidst snow disasters.[44]

X. Offer of Amends

77. The Press Arbitration Act covers the right of reply and the right of correction for those defamed by the news media. Article 14(1) of the Act states: "A person who suffers any damage due to the falsity of a press report on a *factual* allegation … may, within three months after that press report comes to his or her knowledge, require the relevant press organization to report a corrected statement of the details of such press report: *Provided*, That this shall not apply in any case in which six months have elapsed since that report."

41. Constitutional Court, decided on December 26, 2013, 2009Hun-Ma747.
42. Supreme Court, decided on July 8, 2003, 2002Da64384.
43. Supreme Court, decided on September 2, 2011, 2010Do17237.
44. Supreme Court, decided on November 13, 2008, 2008Da53805.

78. Article 16 of the Act provides a right to reply to factual statements for a defamed individual. The application of the right of reply does not hinge on whether the original defamatory news reports were true or false.

XI. Internet Intermediaries

79. The Information and Communications Network Act regulates online defamation as a crime. Article 70(1) of the Act provides:

(1) A person who commits defamation of another person by disclosing a (true) fact to the public through an information and communications network purposely to disparage his/her reputation shall be punished by imprisonment with labor for up to three years or by a fine not exceeding KRW 30 million.
(2) A person who commits defamation of another person by disclosing a false fact to the public through an information and communications network purposely to disparage his/her reputation shall be punished by imprisonment with labor for up to seven years, by suspension of qualification for up to ten years, or by a fine not exceeding KRW 50 million.
(3) The public prosecutor may not prosecute a defamer against the victim's will.

80. Article 44-2 of the Act requires that the information service provider, when received the victim's request, must delete or block the harmful information immediately and then must inform both the requester and the poster of its own action.

81. If the information service provider has difficulty in determining whether such information violated other's rights, the provider has the discretion to block access to the information for thirty days. In addition, the information service provider that attempted to delete or block harmful information may have its liability for damages caused by such information mitigated or discharged.

82. The Information and Communications Network Act has a purpose of providing an effective way for online users to protect their privacy and reputation. If an information service provider that received the user's request did not delete allegedly harmful content, the provider must take liability for defamation or invasion of privacy along with the original poster. As a consequence, the law presents a strong incentive for information service provider to delete injurious information.

83. It has been questioned whether such takedown decision by the information service provider may invade freedom of online speech. The Constitutional Court, however, held that the temporary takedown procedure did not violate online user's freedom of expression.[45] The court reasoned that harmful expression could be spread so quickly and widely that a temporary takedown would be the best way to prevent the spread of defamatory materials. The Constitutional Court stated that the

45. Constitutional Court, decided on May 31, 2012, 2010Hun-Ma88.

importance of protecting the reputation and privacy of the person who challenged the postings would outweigh the complainant's freedom of expression. According to the court, the thirty days of temporary takedown were appropriate to protect the reputation of a potential victim.

84. In 2009, the Supreme Court of Korea made a landmark decision on Internet intermediary's liability. The Supreme Court ruled that Internet intermediary should be liable even when it did not receive any notification from the plaintiff about the existence of defamatory statements. In *Kim v. NHN Corp.*,[46] the plaintiff Kim sued three major Korean Internet intermediaries for online defamation. Kim argued that those Internet intermediaries had disseminated news stories claiming that Kim had betrayed his pregnant ex-girlfriend, which supposedly drove her to commit suicide. Kim also claimed that the Internet intermediaries had facilitated many individual blogs, through which online users disclosed Kim's workplace and phone number resulting in constant harassment. The ISPs responded that they merely distributed news articles originally published by offline news media and that they had legal contracts with news media not to edit or delete news stories at will.

85. The Supreme Court disagreed with ISPs. The court stated that the ISPs performed as more than mere search engines when they received news articles from other news media, stored news information in their database, selected stories for online publication, and eventually distributed news to the public. Hence, the ISPs as news aggregators should be liable just like the offline news media that originally published the precipitating stories. The court went further in holding that even if the ISPs signed contracts with news media not to edit the original stories, the contract applied only between the ISPs and the news media. As a consequence, the contract had no impact on the ISP's liability for defamation.

86. The majority and concurring opinions, however, diverged on whether a defamed person's request to take down a web post or not would be factored as a necessary element in assessing the liability of the ISP. The majority of the court held that since ISPs have been earning enormous profits from the distributing of news information through their web portals, they should pay attention not to deliver harmful information to the public under any circumstances. According to the majority, ISPs should be liable (1) when illegality of the defamatory statement was clear; (2) when the ISP's control over its contents was technically and economically feasible; (3) when the ISP received a notice of defamatory contents on its website; and (4) even if the ISP did not receive any notification, when it obviously knew or had reason to know of the existence of libelous contents under certain circumstances. The majority concluded that an ISP should be responsible for deleting defamatory postings regardless of whether they were notified of the postings or not.

87. The concurring justices disagreed with the majority of the court on the takedown obligations that do not require prior notifications. To balance freedom of speech with reputation, three concurring justices suggested four conditions: (1) a

46. Supreme Court, decided on April 16, 2009, 2008Da53812.

defamed person should request ISPs to delete malicious postings about him/herself; (2) the plaintiff should specify the libelous statements at issue; (3) the illegality of defamation should be evident, though ISPs are not required to prove all elements of defamation to make it actionable; (4) it should be technically and economically feasible for ISPs to eliminate the libelous statements.

XII. Remedies

88. Article 764 of the Civil Act provides a special measure to help the injured party to recover his/her reputation. Under the article, the court may order the defamer to take "measures appropriate" for the injured "either in lieu of or together with provision of compensation." The "measures appropriate" means the retraction of the defamatory statement or publishing court's final decision that the defendant illegally defamed the plaintiff.

89. The right of correction, the right of reply, and the right of further report are also available under the Press Arbitration Act.

XIII. Procedure

90. The Code of Criminal Procedure applies to criminal defamation.

91. The Code of Civil Procedure applies to defamation in civil courts.

92. In order to exercise one's right of reply or correction under the Press Arbitration Act, the claimant must undergo an arbitration procedure and obtain a ruling from the Press Arbitration Commission (PAC).

93. Yet one may directly file a claim for the right of reply or correction under the Civil Code without undergoing the press arbitration procedure. The exercise of such rights does not preclude the victim's separate right to sue for damages.

§4. Insult

94. Insult is a crime when it delivers an expression of derogatory emotion unaccompanied by factual statements that undermine other's reputation.

95. Article 311 of the Criminal Act penalizes insult: "A person who publicly insults another shall be punished by imprisonment or imprisonment without prison labor for not more than one year or by a fine not exceeding two million *won*."

96. In 2013, the Constitutional Court reviewed whether punishment of insult as criminal offense is constitutional or not.[47] The court ruled that punishment does not infringe on freedom of expression, for ordinary citizens with common sense can predict what kind of expression is banned. The dissenting opinion, however, claimed that the scope of elements of insult as a crime is excessively broad. The dissenting judges were concerned that some negative or critical expressions on political or social issues might be considered an insult.

§5. Privacy

I. Protection of Privacy

97. The right to personal information has been strongly protected as a human right. The Korean Constitutional Court stated that the right of personal information would be derived from the right of human dignity and happiness (Article 10) and the right of privacy (Article 17) of the Constitutional Law.[48]

98. In the past, the right of privacy was understood as a legal guarantee to demand the right to be let alone, but it currently covers the right to manage and control information about oneself. The right of privacy became more important as a right of self-determination on personal information, which determines when, where, and to what extent information about oneself can be controlled and utilized by others. Although there are various laws for protecting personal information, the Personal Information Protection Act was enforced in September 2011 as a general law.

99. The Criminal Act and the Civil Act are important sources of law on privacy. Article 316 of the Criminal Code punishes the opening of sealed letters, documents, or drawings. Professionals such as physicians, lawyers, and priests cannot disclose what they have learned in confidence in the course of their professional work.[49] Likewise, the Postal Services Act forbids postal employees to reveal any private matters that may have come to their knowledge.[50] Intrusion into a private home of another violates the Criminal Act.[51]

100. Invasion of privacy is similar to defamation as a tort under the Civil Act. Article 750 states: "Any person who causes damage to or inflicts injuries on another person by an unlawful act intentionally or negligently must make compensation for damages arising therefrom." Article 751 allows a damage award to a person who has suffered mental anguish because of his privacy being invaded.

47. Constitutional Court, decided on June 27, 2013, 2012Hun-Ba37.
48. Constitutional Court, decided on May 26, 2005, 99Hun-Ma513.
49. Criminal Act, Art. 317.
50. Postal Service Act, Art. 3.
51. Criminal Act, Art. 319.

101. The Press Arbitration Act prohibits the invasion of privacy by the press, stating that "the press shall not violate any right to … privacy, portrait, name, voice, dialogue, works, personal documents, any other personal worth, etc."[52] Article 5-2 of the Press Arbitration Act recognizes the personal right of the deceased.

102. Privacy can be invoked as a statutory ground for exemption to an individual's right to access government records. The Act on Disclosure of Information by Public Agencies contains an exception to release information from a government agency if the informational disclosure may violate an individual's private life.[53] Similarly, the Act on Protection of Personal Information Maintained by Public Agencies limits access to computerized personal information if its inspection violates the privacy of others unjustifiably.[54]

103. Courts have protected a public figure's right of privacy. In 2001, the Seoul High Court held that public figures still have an "inalienable zone of private life," even though more information of public figures should be open to the public:

> A private sphere such as a public figure's family relations can be publicized to a certain extent. But the sexual relationship between a man and a woman falls within the ultimate and inviolable realm of human liberty that is absolutely protected. Thus, the farther away the invaded space of privacy moves from … the public, the thicker the shield against invasion becomes.[55]

104. In this case, a famous woman anchor's divorce is not absolutely safeguarded against news reporting, the appellate court stated, her protection against the gossip about her sexual relationship is more warranted than against the canard about her family relations, marriage, or divorce. The court further considered the challenged news articles in the case merely a "sensational curiosity" about the plaintiff as a celebrity and not a matter of "legitimate public concern."

II. Right of Personal Information on the Internet

105. Two acts have protected the right of personal information on the Internet. First, the Information and Communications Network Act provides online users with a right to delete harmful information. Article 44-2 of the Information and Communications Network Act states that when someone invades other's privacy or defames another person, the victim may request the information service provider to delete harmful contents or to post a rebuttal statement. Article 44-3 allows the information service provider to block access to online posting arbitrarily even when the provider did not receive any request or notification from the victim.

52. Press Arbitration Act, Art. 5(1).
53. The Act on Disclosure of Information by Public Agencies, Art. 9(1)6.
54. Act on Protection of Personal Information Maintained by Public Agencies, Art. 3.
55. Seoul High Court, decided on May 31, 2001, 2000Na11098.

106. Second, the Personal Information Act provides citizens with a right to delete or correct personal information. A person may request a manager of personal information to allow his or her inspection of his or her own personal information[56] and then may request the information manager to correct or delete such information.[57] So long as other law does not require the information manager to collect such personal information, the manager must correct or delete information immediately. Also, a person may request the information manager to suspend managing his or her personal information.[58]

56. Personal Information Act, Art. 35.
57. *Ibid.*, Art. 36.
58. *Ibid.*, Art. 37.

Chapter 4. Right of Reply

107. The right of reply was adopted in 1990 by the Basic Press Act to balance press freedom with the right of reputation. In 1991, the Constitutional Court held that "a right to reply gives the injured person an opportunity to refute the factual reports by the press, thereby protecting his right to personality."[59] The Korean Supreme Court also recognized in 1991 that the right of reply did not violate constitutional provision of freedom of the press while providing a victim with an "equal weapon" against the media.[60]

108. The Press Arbitration Act enacted in 2005 aims to make freedom of the press compatible with public responsibilities of the press by establishing an effective remedial system including conciliation or arbitration to settle disputes. The Press Arbitration Act applies to Internet news service and Internet multimedia broadcasting as well as the traditional press.[61]

109. Article 14 of the Press Arbitration Act provides a right of correction to a victim who suffers any damage due to the falsity of a press report. The victim may require the press and the ISPs to report a corrected statement of the details of such report. This should be requested within three months after the victim recognized the false allegations and within six months after the press report was published.

110. Article 15(4) states that the press may refuse a request for correction or contradictory statements if any of the following events occur:

(1) Where there is no legitimate interest of an aggrieved party in exercising any right to require the press organization to report a corrected statement.
(2) Where the details of a report on a corrected statement required of the press organization are clearly contrary to fact.
(3) Where the details of a report on a corrected statement required of the press organization are clearly illegal.
(4) Where the details of a report on a corrected statement required of the press organization are only for a commercial advertisement.
(5) Where the details of a report on a corrected statement required of the press organization are related to a factual report on a public meeting of the State, a local government or public organization and on a public trial of a court.

111. Article 16 states that the victim of the press report may require the press to report a contradictory statement of the details of that press report. This request of contradictory statements is similar to the concept of right of reply, for it provides the victim an opportunity to contradict the press. Such request for a contradictory statement to the press shall be made, irrespective of any intention, negligence or illegality of the press and regardless of whether or not the details of the original

59. Constitutional Court, decided on September 16, 1991, 89Hunma165.
60. Supreme Court, decided on January 17, 1991, 90Daka25468.
61. Press Arbitration Act, Art. 5.

report are true. Therefore, even if the press had no intention or negligence of its report and the press' report was legitimate, the alleged victim may request a contradictory statement to the press. Further, the alleged victim may request a contradictory statement even when the details of the original report are true.

112. Article 17 stipulates a right to request a further report to the press. A person reported as a suspected offender or a criminal may require the press to make a further report on the fact that the criminal procedure with respect to him/her was terminated by the final judgment of acquittal. The further report shall include an explanation or elucidation necessary for restoring infringed reputation of the requester.

Chapter 5. Access to Public Information

§1. Public Documents and Meetings

113. Although the Constitution has no specific provision on the right to information, the Constitutional Court has recognized the implied right to know as a constitutional right.[62] The Official Information Disclosure Act, which was originally enacted in 1996, protects the access to information as well. Article 1 of the Official Information Disclosure Act proclaims its purpose: "The purpose of this Act is to guarantee people's rights to know and to secure people's participation in state affairs and the transparency of the operation of state affairs, establishing the necessary matters concerning the public requests for the disclosure of information kept and controlled by public institutions and for the obligations of public institutions to disclose such information."

114. Every citizen has a right to request information disclosure under this Act. Foreigners may also file information disclosure request to the government bodies and public institutions that are subject to the law. Yet foreigners' request must comply with a relevant presidential decree.[63]

115. According to Article 2(1), information is defined as matters recorded in documents, drawings, pictures, films, tapes, slides, and other media corresponding thereto that are made or acquired and managed by public institutions for the performance of their duties. Public institutions, which are obliged to disclose information, are (1) state agencies, (2) local governments, (3) public institutions, and (4) other institutions prescribed by Presidential Decree. State agencies include the National Assembly, courts, the Constitutional Court, the National Election Commission, central administrative agencies, and other governmental committees.[64]

116. Article 3 requires that public institutions must disclose "any information" kept and managed by those institutions in an active manner to ensure people's right to know. This Act shall not apply to any information collected or prepared by agencies, which take charge of information related to national security and security work for the purpose of analyzing information related to national security.[65]

117. Public institutions are required to actively endeavor to disclose information for people's right to know. Public institutions should decide on the detailed scope of information disclosure and period, timing, and methods for such disclosure in advance and must officially announce any of the following information:[66]

---

62. Constitutional Court, decided on September 4, 1989, 88Hunma22.
63. Official Information Disclosure Act, Art. 5.
64. *Ibid.*, Art. 2(3).
65. *Ibid.*, Art. 4.
66. *Ibid.*, Art. 7.

(1) Information pertaining to any policy that has significant effects on people's life.
(2) Information pertaining to any project that required a large-scale budget, including works undertaken in accordance with the State policy.
(3) Information required for administrative supervision, including details of budget execution and result of project evaluation.
(4) Other information prescribed by the heads of public institutions.

118. The Official Information Disclosure Act sets down eight grounds of exemptions to information disclosures. Article 9 states:

(1) Information specifically exempted by the Act and other laws.
(2) Information relating to national security, national defense, unification, diplomatic relations, etc.
(3) Information harmful to the protection of individuals' lives, physical safety, and properties.
(4) Information relating to ongoing trials, crime investigation and prevention, institution and maintenance of indictments, or the execution of sentence and security disposition.
(5) Information relating to audit, supervision, inspection, tests, regulations, tendering contract, the development of technology, the management of personal affairs, decision-making processes and internal review processes, etc.
(6) Information relating to resident registration numbers and other private information of individuals.
(7) Information relating to management and trade secrets of corporations, organizations, or individuals.
(8) Information relating to real estate and the acts of cornering and hoarding real estate.

119. A public institution shall decide whether or not they disclose the requested information within ten days from the date when such request is received. If a public institution is unable to make a decision within ten days, the public institution may extend the period for up to ten days.[67] Particularly, Article 11(3) states that when any public institution is aware that the requested information pertains, in whole or in part, to a third party, the public institution shall inform the third party of the fact without delay and may, if necessary, hear that party's opinion on the information.

120. When a public institution decides not to disclose information, it must "promptly" notify the requester in writing of its nondisclosure decision.[68] In the case of a refusal of access, the Act requires that the reasons for the decision be explained to the requester. Even if the third party refuses to authorize access to information that the third party already supplied to the government, the public body

67. *Ibid.*, Art. 11.
68. *Ibid.*, Art. 13.

can make its own decision on whether to allow access to the information. The third parties cannot exercise a veto over the freedom of information decisions by government authorities.

121. The denial of access requests may be appealed administratively. The requester may ask the government agency to reconsider its initial denial of his or her information disclosure request. The internal appeal may be filed within thirty days after the requester is notified of the agency's decision to reject his or her request in whole or in part.[69] The internal appeal must be decided within seven days. If an agency cannot respond to the internal appeal due to unavoidable circumstances, the agency has an extended deadline of seven days.

122. If an agency's reply to the appeal is not acceptable, the requester may use an administrative appeal under the Administrative Appeals Act.[70] The administrative appeal may be filed without following the internal appeals under the Official Information Disclosure Act.

123. Where an applicant is dissatisfied with a decision made by a public institution in connection with information disclosure, or when no decision is made on disclosure of information even after the lapse of twenty days after the request for information disclosure was made, he/she may file for an administrative litigation.[71]

§2. Court Hearings and Documents

I. The Open Justice Principle and Access to the Courts

124. The Constitution protects a right to a fast and open trial. Article 27(1) of the Constitution states that all citizens shall have the right of trial in conformity with the law and by judges. Article 27(3) declares: "All citizens shall have the right to a speedy trial. The accused shall have the right to a public trial without delay in the absences of justifiable reasons to the contrary." Although the Constitution does not have an article relating to fair trial, the right to fair trial derives from Article 27.

125. Article 109 of the Constitution proclaims: "Trials and decisions of the courts shall be open to the public." This right to open trial, however, is not absolute. Trials may be closed to the public by a court decision "when there is a danger that such trials may undermine the national security or disturb public safety and order, or be harmful to public morals."[72] Similarly, Article 57 of the Court Organization Act says, "hearing and judgment of a trial shall be open to the public," but the trial may be closed to the public "if it might endanger the national security, public peace and order, or good public moral."

69. *Ibid.,* Art. 18(1).
70. *Ibid.,* Art. 19.
71. *Ibid.,* Art. 20(1).
72. Constitution, Art. 109.

126. Anybody who wants to record on videotape, take a photograph, and relay broadcasting in court should get permission from the presiding judge under Article 59 of the Court Organization Act. Therefore, the press is allowed to take pictures or film in court only when the judge authorizes. Such permission is rarely given to the press.

127. The Supreme Court Rule of Photographing in Court details how to get the permission. The person who wants to take pictures or films has to submit a permission form by a day before, filling out his/her name and affiliation, purpose, time and object.[73] The presiding judge may permit such pictures or films only when the complainant and the defendant agree. Nonetheless, the judge may give permission on public interest even if the complainant and the defendant disagree.[74] If someone takes pictures or films in court without permission, the presiding judge may order them to leave the court. Taking pictures of and other activities involving the accused are allowed after handcuffs have been taken off. Taking pictures of and other activities involving juveniles should be handled in a manner such that their names, age, occupation, and appearance are not recognizable.[75]

128. In 2014, after the tragic *Sewol* ferry disaster, the Supreme Court Rule of Photographing in Court was revised to justify electronic access to proceedings in an off-site location. According to Article 6 of the Supreme Court Rule, photographing, recording and broadcasting in court is exceptionally permitted to access in off-site location (1) when those concerned with the court proceedings outnumber the number of people that the courtroom can accommodate; and (2) when a disaster has claimed a number of people, and the parties in interest, victims, or those representing the deceased have long distance travel difficulties in attending the trial.

II. Access to Criminal Courts

129. The Police Rule for Protection of Human Rights has not allowed the publishing of the personal information of suspects since 2005. In 2010, the Act on Special Cases Concerning the Punishment of Specific Violent Crimes was revised to allow disclosure of suspect's personal information in certain limited circumstances.

130. The Act on Special Cases Concerning the Punishment of Specific Violent Crimes prescribes special cases concerning disclosure of personal information under Article 8(2). A public prosecutor and a police officer may disclose personal information such as face, name and age on a suspect of a specific violent crime, if all the following requirements are satisfied:

(1) It shall be a specific violent crime that has been committed in a cruel way and has brought material damage.

73. Supreme Court Rule of Photographing in Court, Art. 4(1).
74. *Ibid.*, Art. 4(2).
75. *Ibid.*, Art. 4(5).

(2) Sufficient evidence shall exist to prove that the criminal suspect has committed such crime.
(3) Disclosure shall be required for the public good only, such as the guarantee of the people's right to know, the prevention of recidivism by a criminal suspect, and the prevention of crimes.
(4) A criminal suspect shall not be a juvenile referred to in subparagraph 1 of Article 2 of the Juvenile Protection Act.

131. When the prosecutor or police officer makes a disclosure of private information, he/she should make a careful decision considering the criminal suspect's human rights and should not abuse such disclosure.[76] Following the revised law, the media can reveal a serious suspect's name, face and age when the police inform the press of such private information.

132. Article 126 of the Criminal Act punishes police, prosecutors, or other persons who are involved in activities concerning investigation of crimes when they reveal the facts of a suspected crime. In addition, Article 198(2) of the Criminal Procedure Act states that each prosecutor, judicial police officer and other persons whose duties involve investigation should respect the human rights of a criminal suspect and should keep the secret known to him/her in the course of investigation.

133. Several other laws prohibit media from revealing the identification of the accused. For example, Article 10 of the Family Litigation Act states: "With respect to any case which is under proceedings in, or settled by the family court, any facts or photographs to the level sufficient to surmise the identity from the name, age, occupation, appearance, etc., shall not be printed in any newspaper, magazine, or other publications, or broadcast."[77]

III. Access to Civil Courts

134. Law does not restrict news media from accessing and reporting on civil court's procedure. Given the constitutional guarantee of open court proceedings as a right for the public, restrictions should be the exception.

135. But several countervailing interests are recognized constitutionally and statutorily as justifications for limiting public access to trials. The Court Organization Act allows the presiding judge of a trial to bar any person who might endanger the dignity and order of the court, and he may take necessary measures to maintain order in court.[78] Further, no one may videotape, photograph, or broadcast court proceedings without the permission of the presiding judge.[79]

76. Act on Special Cases Concerning the Punishment of Specific Violent Crimes, Art. 8(2).
77. Family Litigation Act, Art. 10.
78. Court Organization Act, Art. 58(2).
79. *Ibid.*, Art. 59.

IV. Contempt of Court

136. Contempt of court means a form of disturbance that may prevent the function of the court. In this case, the judge may impose fines or jail time on any person who commits contempt of court.

137. The Criminal Act punishes a person who threatens or disturbs the legal authorities in the courtroom. Article 138 of Criminal Act states:

> A person who insults a court or a parliamentary chamber for the purpose of interfering with or threatening the judgement of the court or the deliberation of the National Assembly shall be punished by imprisonment not more than three years or by a fine not exceeding seven million *won*.

138. Similarly, Article 58 of the Court Organization Act stipulates that the presiding judge may prohibit a person who is disrespectful or order him/her to leave the court:

(1) Order in the court shall be maintained by the presiding judge.
(2) The presiding judge may prohibit any person who might endanger the dignity and order of the court from entering the court or may order him/her to leave the court. The presiding judge may issue orders necessary for maintaining order in the court.

139. These laws, however, do not punish a person who refuses to respond to subpoena, to testify or to provide certain information. There is no statutory regulation in case of rejecting testimony in court.

V. Reporting Restrictions

140. The Constitution declares the "presumption of innocence" principle under Article 27(4): "The accused shall be presumed innocent until a judgment of guilt has been pronounced." Consequently, journalists are supposed not to reveal personal information of the suspect until proven guilty. If a journalist reveals personal information of the suspect, such as name or photo, the journalist might be sued for the invasion of privacy or defamation under the Civil Act or the Criminal Act.

141. For instance, KBS news reported in 1990 that a wife and her friend were arrested for attempting to murder her husband. However, the Supreme Court in 1992 ruled that the suspects were not guilty. After the Supreme Court's decision, the acquitted suspects sued KBS news reporters for defamation. The reporters claimed that their news reporting was based on the police officer's news briefing and did not recognize that the suspicion of attempted murder was false.[80]

80. Supreme Court, decided on July 14, 1998, 96Da17257.

142. In 1998, the Supreme Court held that if suspects are ordinary individuals, not public figures, the public does not have the right to know about personal information of the suspects.[81] The court reasoned that there is no reasonable public interest in identifying the private figures in a media report.

143. Similarly, the Supreme Court ruled in 2007 that there is no right to know about identification of a private figure. In the case, Yonhap News Agency delivered a false report that a medical doctor allowed his staff to compound drugs without authorization. The court ruled that the news agency defamed the doctor and thus the news agency must compensate the damage for disclosing his name.[82]

81. *Ibid.*
82. Supreme Court, decided on July 12, 2007, 2006Da165620.

Chapter 6. Press Council

144. The Press Ethics Committee is a self-regulatory body by the media themselves. It was founded in 1961 by the Korean Association of Newspapers, the Korea News Editors' Association, and the Journalists Association of Korea.

145. The Press Ethics Committee oversees the newspaper ethics code that sets out the freedom and responsibility of the press. Also, the Press Ethics Committee lays down the code of ethics for reporting suicide, the rules for reporting disaster, and the rules for reporting opinion poll for the general election.

146. The code of ethics for reporting suicide states that the press should abstain from reporting suicides, except for cases related to public interest. In addition, the code says journalists must not include excessive details about methods and location of suicides, while protecting privacy of the suicide victims and his/her surviving family. Journalists are required not to reveal the name of the suicide victims if the case does not involve substantial public interests.

147. The rule for reporting disaster states its purpose as preventing the confusion of media reporting about disasters such as floods, storms, heavy snow, fire, explosion, and infectious diseases. Article 15 of the rule recommends that excessive emotional expressions or repetitive reports of sensational scenes should be avoided. Article 16 states that media should abstain from using offensive, frightening, or irritating words for news reporting. According to Article 18, the media should not infringe on the victim's honor, privacy, and psychological stability. For the interviews with victims, the reporter is required to pay special attention to questions and interview time for protecting the victims.

Part III. Regulation of Audiovisual Media (Broadcasting)

Chapter 1. Public Service Broadcasting

§1. The Concept and Mission of Public Service Broadcasting

148. The concept of public service broadcasting is not legally defined, but it is conceived as a broadcasting that serves the public rather than focusing on commercial practices and profit-seeking.

149. In South Korea, public service broadcasting includes the KBS, MBC, and EBS. Article 43 of the Broadcasting Act states that the KBS was established "as the State's key broadcasting in order to fix a fair and sound broadcast culture, and to efficiently implement the broadcasts for home and abroad."[83] As a representative public service broadcasting in South Korea, according to Article 44 of the Act, the KBS is expected to "bring into reality the objectives and public responsibility of broadcasting, and the impartiality and public interest nature of broadcasting."[84] It is noteworthy that the government paid the full amount of capital of the KBS.

150. In 1969, MBC started its television broadcasting.[85] MBC has been conceived as a public service broadcaster because its largest shareholder, Foundation for Broadcast Culture (FBC), was established by a special law that intends to oversee MBC to fulfill its public responsibilities.[86] Thus, MBC's mission includes promoting "democratic, fair, and sound broadcasting culture as well as enhancement of public welfare."[87] As a public broadcasting entity, EBS has served as the only major educational television and radio network in South Korea, proclaiming itself as the world's best "education specialized media group."[88]

83. Broadcasting Act, Art. 43. Please note that the English version of legal provisions cited in Part III can be accessed at, https://elaw.klri.re.kr/eng_service/main.do. The translation is provided by the Korea Legislation Research Institute & Korea Law Translation Center.
84. Broadcasting Act, Art. 44.
85. *See* http://with.mbc.co.kr/about/history/index.html.
86. *See* Yeong-Man Jeon, *Broadcasting and Telecommunications Law Handbook* 174 (2015).
87. *See* http://www.fbc.or.kr/Introduction/Eng/Mission.
88. *See* http://global.ebs.co.kr/eng/about/vision?tabVal=strategy.

§2. THE ORGANIZATION OF PUBLIC SERVICE BROADCASTING

151. KBS is considered a key public broadcasting in South Korea. KBS launched its first radio broadcasting in 1927 and its television broadcasting in 1961 and completed its transfer to digital broadcasting in 2012.[89] As of August 2020, KBS has eighteen regional stations, eleven overseas bureaus, and eight subsidiary companies, including KBS Media which manages a range of business operations.[90] Channels of KBS include: (1) Radio: Radio1, Radio2, Radio3, Global Korean Network, FM1 and FM2; (2) Terrestrial TV: 1TV and 2TV; (3) Cable TV: KBS Drama, KBS Joy, KBS Sports, KBS W, KBS Kids, and KBS Prime; (4) Terrestrial DMB: U-KBS Star, U-KBS Music, U-KBS Heart, and U-KBS Clover; and (5) International Broadcasting: KBS World TV and KBS World Radio.[91]

152. Article 46 of the Broadcasting Act states the following:

> (1) [KBS] shall have a board of directors as the highest decision-making body for the management of [KBS] in order to guarantee the independence and public nature of [KBS]. (2) The board of directors shall be comprised of eleven directors, including the Chairman of the board of directors. (3) The directors shall be recommended by the Korea Communications Commission in consideration of their typicality of different fields, and appointed by the President. (4) The Chairman of the board of directors shall be elected by the board of directors by mutual vote … .[92]

153. The meetings of the board of directors are supposed to be open to the public with several exceptions laid out in the Act. The Broadcasting Act declares that KBS is independent of the government. However, some critics have cast doubt on that claim, observing that the president of KBS is appointed by the President of Korea.[93]

154. According to Article 50 of the Broadcasting Act, the President of Korea appoints the president of KBS based on the recommendation of the board of directors, and the president of KBS appoints the vice president(s) and managing directors.[94] The recommendation of the board of directors is needed when appointing the vice president(s).[95] The auditor of KBS is appointed by the Korea Communications

89. *See* http://english.kbs.co.kr/about/overview_01.html.
90. *See* http://english.kbs.co.kr/about/overview_01.html.
91. *See* http://english.kbs.co.kr/about/overview_03.html.
92. Broadcasting Act, Art. 46.
93. *See* http://www.pdjournal.com/news/articleView.html?idxno=56911. According to Art. 50(2) of the Broadcasting Act, "the president shall be appointed by President upon a proposal by the board of directors. In such cases, the president shall undergo a personnel hearings conducted by the National Assembly."
94. Broadcasting Act, Art. 50.
95. *Ibid.*

Commission (KCC) on the recommendation of the board of directors. The term of directorship is three years, with the possibility of reappointment.[96]

155. Conditions for disqualification of directors of KBS are spelled out in Article 48 of the Broadcasting Act.[97] The personnel of KBS can be dismissed by the president of KBS under the conditions prescribed in the articles of incorporation.

§3. The Financing of Public Service Broadcasting

156. The primary source of revenue for the KBS is a license fee.[98] As of 2019, the license fees cover about 46% of the total finances needed to run and operate the institution.[99] Article 56 of the Broadcasting Act states that "Expenses of the [KBS] shall be met by the television broadcast receiving fees collected under Article 64, but such expenses may be covered by revenues prescribed by President Decree, such as revenues from commercials, if necessary for properly performing its affairs as intended."[100] In 2008, in its television broadcast receiving fees case, the Constitutional Court of Korea found that Article 64 of the Broadcasting Act is constitutional.[101]

157. Article 64 of the Broadcasting Act states the following:

> Any person who possesses a television receiver (hereinafter referred to as "TV set") in order to receive television broadcasts shall register the TV set with the System, and pay a television broadcast receiving fee (hereinafter referred to as the "receiving fees") under the conditions as prescribed by Presidential Decree: *Provided*, That with regard to the TV sets as prescribed by Presidential Decree, their registration may be exempted, or all or part of the receiving fees may be exempted or reduced.[102]

158. The largest portion of MBC's revenue is made up of advertising sales.[103] In 2013, the combined revenue of advertising and sponsorship accounted for 67.7% of the total revenue of MBC (including eighteen regional MBCs).[104] It may be argued that categorizing MBC as public service broadcasting is questionable, given that the advertising revenue of public broadcasting should be small.[105] However, the

---

96. *See* http://english.kbs.co.kr/about/overview_02.html.
97. Broadcasting Act, Art. 48.
98. *See* http://open.kbs.co.kr/index.html?sname=finance&stype=info .
99. *Ibid.*
100. Broadcasting Act, Art. 56.
101. 2006Hun-Ba70, February 28, 2008.
102. Broadcasting Act, Art. 64.
103. *See* Yeong-Man Jeon, *Broadcasting and Telecommunications Law Handbook* 176 (2015).
104. *Ibid.*
105. *Ibid.*

FBC, the largest shareholder of MBC, holds 70% of MBC's stake.[106] As a not-for-profit statutory corporation, the FBC supervises MBC. Thus, MBC is expected to promote broadcasting and fulfill public responsibilities, and there is little need to pursue private shareholders' profit or maximization of sales. However, the degree of independence of financial resources is low compared to KBS.[107]

159. As a public broadcasting entity, EBS receives a small portion of license fees collected by the KBS as well as government subsidies.[108] Article 68 of the Broadcasting Act states that "[KBS] may use the receiving fees … for the support as a revenue to the [EBS] under the Korea Educational Broadcasting System Act under the conditions as prescribed by Presidential Decree."[109] In 2012, according to EBS, textbook sales, publications, and ad revenues from a wide range of its platforms occupied 72.1% of its revenue.[110]

106. *Ibid.*
107. *Ibid.*
108. *Ibid.*, at 179.
109. Broadcasting Act, Art. 68.
110. *See* http://global.ebs.co.kr/eng/about/report.

Chapter 2. Private Broadcasting

§1. Different Categories of Private Broadcasters

160. According to Article 2 of the Broadcasting Act, broadcasting means "planning, programming or producing broadcast programs, and transmitting them to the general public ... through telecommunication facilities ... ".[111] Categories of broadcasting include (1) television broadcasting, (2) radio broadcasting, (3) datacasting, and (4) DBM.[112] It is important to note that datacasting through the Internet is excluded in this category.[113] In South Korea, "broadcasting business" includes the following categories: terrestrial broadcasting, CATV broadcasting, satellite broadcasting, and program-providing business. These business operators should obtain a license under Article 9 of the Broadcasting Act.

161. Internet broadcasting is regulated by the Internet Multimedia Broadcast Services Act.[114] According to this Act, Internet multimedia broadcasting refers to "broadcasting which provides various content, including data, picture, voice, sounds and electronic commerce, including real-time broadcast programs, to users through television receivers, while a two-way Internet protocol ensures consistency in the quality of service, using a broadband integrated services digital network (excluding telecommunications line facilities for services using frequencies allocated to conduct facilities-based service under Article 10(1) 1 of the Radio Waves Act, regardless of whether the facilities are self-owned or leased)."[115]

162. When it comes to radio broadcasting, there are many radio stations, including standard radio stations, such as KBS, MBC, SBS, and EBS. As noted earlier, SBS radio is considered private broadcasting. Christian Broadcasting System (CBS) is the first independent commercial radio station in South Korea, and it runs Christian programs.[116] It is worth mentioning that there exist other religious programming broadcasters and specialized broadcasters, such as Traffic Broadcasting System (TBS). As a representative English broadcasting station established by the Korea International Broadcasting Foundation, a nonprofit organization in South Korea, Arirang TV/Radio provides news and entertainment programs on Korea to global audiences interested in Korean culture and society.[117]

163. In South Korea, the first television station, HLKZ-TV, began its broadcasting in 1956.[118] Several private broadcasters emerged in the 1960s. As a commercial broadcaster in South Korea, SBS was founded in 1990.[119] SBS initially broadcasted

111. Broadcasting Act, Art. 2.
112. *Ibid.*
113. *Ibid.*
114. *See* https://elaw.klri.re.kr/kor_service/lawView.do?hseq=46591&lang=ENG.
115. Internet Multimedia Broadcast Service Act, Art. 2.1.
116. *See* http://about.cbs.co.kr/eng/cbs.asp.
117. *See* http://www.arirang.com/prroom/about_arirangn1.asp?sys_lang=Eng.
118. *See* https://theme.archives.go.kr//next/koreaOfRecord/television.do.
119. *See* http://www.sbsmedia.co.kr/history.jsp.

its program in Seoul and neighboring areas. But SBS later established its national network that includes Gangwon No. 1 Broadcasting (G1), Taejon Broadcasting Corporation (TJB), Cheongju Broadcasting Corporation (CJB), Jeonju Television Corporation (JTV), Kwangju Broadcasting Corporation (KBC), Taegu Broadcasting Corporation (TBC), Korea New Network (KNN), Ulsan Broadcasting Corporation (UBC), and Jeju Free International City Broadcasting System (JIBS).[120] SBS provides these regional television and radio broadcasting companies with some of its programs. It should be noted that there exist other commercial broadcasters that do not belong to the SBS network such as OBS Gyeongin TV.

164. Korea has witnessed the launch of several nationwide general cable TV networks that have programming freedom like terrestrial broadcasting companies. Those general cable TV networks include JoongAng Ilbo's JTBC, Chosun Ilbo's TV Chosun, Maeil Kyungje's MBN, and Dong-A Ilbo's Channel A.[121] According to Article 2 of the Broadcasting Act, general programming means "an act of organizing the broad cast programs in order to form a mutual harmony between the diverse broadcast fields such as news reports, culture and entertainment."[122]

§2. Licencing Requirements

165. Obtaining a license from the KCC is required to run a terrestrial broadcasting business in South Korea.[123] Based on the Radio Waves Act that governs the opening of wireless stations, the KCC requests a technical evaluation to the Minister of Science, ICT and Future Planning. In issuing a license, the results of the evaluation should be reflected.[124] According to Article 10 of the Broadcasting Act, when reviewing licencing requests, the KCC should consider the following criteria for evaluation: (1) "Possibility of realizing a public responsibility, impartiality and public interest of broadcasting," (2) "Appropriateness of the planning, programming and production plans of broadcasting programs," (3) "Regional, social and cultural necessity and validity," (4) "Appropriateness of management plans such as the organization and manpower operation," (5) "Financial and technical capability," (6) "Support plans for the advancement of broadcasting," and (7) "Other matters necessary for conducting the business."[125] The Broadcasting Act also mandates that when conducting an evaluation for licencing approval, the Minister of Science, ICT and Future Planning or the KCC should solicit and openly hear viewers' opinions. The KCC conducts broadcasting evaluation on a yearly basis, and a renewed license or renewed approval should reflect the evaluation results.[126]

120. *See* Yeong-Man Jeon, *Broadcasting and Telecommunications Law Handbook* 181 (2015).
121. *See* https://www.korea.kr/news/policyNewsView.do?newsId=148723323.
122. Broadcasting Act, Art. 2.
123. *Ibid.*, Art. 9.
124. *See* https://elaw.klri.re.kr/kor_service/lawView.do?hseq=50184&lang=ENG.
125. Broadcasting Act, Art. 10.
126. Korea Communications Commission, Annual Report (2016).

Chapter 3. Program Standards

§1. Impartiality

166. Article 6 of the Broadcasting Act requires broadcasters to respect impartiality and public interest. Article 6(9) states that "A broadcast shall, in particular announcing the policies, etc. of the Government or a specific group, strive to provide an equal opportunity to other groups having different opinions, and also endeavor to maintain a balance in organizing the broadcast programs with respect to each party of political interests."[127] It is worth noting that having in place regulations that ensure program impartiality does not automatically guarantee the proper functioning of those regulations. Union members of KBS and MBC went on large-scale strikes in September 2017, demanding the resignations of then presidents of KBS and MBC, respectively.[128] One of the leading causes for the union strikes was the alleged censoring of employees and programs, and the executives' political bias tilted toward conservative causes.[129]

§2. Cultural Diversity

167. Entertainment programs cannot occupy more than 50% of programing hours of general television and radio broadcasters.[130] In addition to other programming requirements, the government imposes a limit on foreign content on broadcasters. The Broadcasting Act requires that domestically produced movies, animations, and music programs are broadcast above a specified ratio. Specific quota requirements are prescribed by the Enforcement Decree of the Broadcasting Act.[131] For example, the range of domestic quota for terrestrial broadcasters and terrestrial rerun cable networks is from 60% up to 80% of the total broadcasting hours of the relevant channel for every half year.[132] For satellite and cable operators, the

127. Broadcasting Act, Art. 6(9).
128. *See* https://thediplomat.com/2017/09/strife-in-south-korea-over-politics-in-public-broadcasting/.
129. *See* http://www.koreaherald.com/view.php?ud=20171107000825.
130. Article 50(1) of the Enforcement Decree of the Broadcasting Act states: "A broadcasting business operator that engages in general programming shall ensure that the broadcast programs related to news reports, broadcast programs related to culture, and broadcast programs related to entertainment are well-coordinated under the former part of Article 69(3) of the Act, and the specific standards for such programming shall be as follows: 1. In cases of TV broadcast programs or radio broadcast programs, the broadcasting hours of those related to entertainment shall not exceed 50/100 of the total monthly broadcasting hours of the relevant; 2. In cases of datacasting programs, those related to entertainment shall not exceed 60/100 of the total monthly broadcasting content of the relevant channel."
131. Article 57 of the Enforcement Decree of the Broadcasting Act regulates programming of domestically-produced broadcast programs.
132. *Ibid.*

range is 40–70.[133] And for programming providers, the range is 20–50.[134] In addition, to ensure diversity in the reception of international cultures, it is stipulated that films, animations and popular music imported from one foreign country should not exceed a specified ratio—80/100.[135]

§3. PROTECTION OF MINORS (INDECENCY AND VIOLENCE)

168. The Broadcasting Act requires that broadcasters should not promote obscenity, indecency, or violence that adversely affects the soundness of family life and the guidance of children and adolescents.[136] As a media regulation agency, the KCC has the responsibility for protecting youth and children.[137] Accordingly, it has established rules for classifying programs, which appear on a television screen corner while broadcast programs air. There are five types of ratings: all age groups, 7 and over, 12 and over, 15 and over, and 19 and over.[138]

§4. HUMAN DIGNITY

169. Article 35 of the Broadcasting Act mandates protections for viewers' rights by requiring the KCC to establish a "Viewers' Rights Protection Committee."[139] The main task of the Committee is to collect the viewers' opinions about broadcasts and Internet multimedia broadcasting. In order to help people with disabilities access broadcast programs, broadcasting business operators should provide sign language broadcasting service, closed-caption subtitles, screen commentaries, among others, to a certain ratio.[140] In addition, based on Article 7(2) of Framework Act on Broadcasting Communications Development, "the Korea Communications Commission shall establish and implement a specific plan for supporting minorities or the socially marginalized in order to prevent them from being unfavorably treated or alienated in broadcasting communications on the grounds of their economic, geographic, or physical differences."[141]

---

133. *Ibid.*
134. *Ibid.*
135. Article 57(5) of the Enforcement Decree of the Broadcasting Act states: "Pursuant to Article 71(4) of the [Broadcasting] Act, a broadcasting business entity shall program movies, animations and popular music produced by a certain country among movies, animations and popular music imported from foreign countries, not more than the ratio publicly announced by the Korea Communications Commission, within the limit of 80 percent of the total broadcasting hours of imported movies, animations and popular music of the relevant channel for every half year."
136. Broadcasting Act, Art. 5. Article 5(5) of the Act states: "A broadcast shall not promote lewdness, decadence or violence which has a negative influence on a sound family life and on a guidance of children and juveniles."
137. *See* https://kcc.go.kr/user.do?mode=view&page=A02020400&dc=K00000001&boardId=1006&boardSeq=25167.
138. *Ibid.*
139. Broadcasting Act, Art. 35.
140. *Ibid.*, Art. 69.
141. Framework Act on Broadcasting Commissions Development, Art. 7(2).

§5. Right of Reply

170. The right of reply that allows individuals and organizations to refute a press report is recognized by the Act on Press Arbitration and Remedies, etc. for Damage Caused by Press Reports.[142] As a statutory right, the right of reply is only applied to factual allegations.[143] A person whose reputational right has been damaged by a press report or broadcast program can request the same medium where the defamatory remark was made to report a contradictory statement.[144] This request can be made regardless of whether the original report was true.[145] A person who claims his/her right of reply needs to exercise the right within three months after the press report comes to his/her knowledge and six months after the relevant press report.[146]

---

142. *See* https://elaw.klri.re.kr/kor_service/lawView.do?hseq=24492&lang=ENG.
143. Act on Press Arbitration and Remedies, etc. for Damage Caused by Press Reports, Art. 16.
144. *Ibid.*
145. *Ibid.*
146. Act on Press Arbitration and Remedies, etc. for Damage Caused by Press Reports, Art. 14 & Art. 16.

Chapter 4. Political Broadcasting

§1. Rules on Political Independence of Broadcasters

171. Article 4 of the Broadcasting Act protects freedom and independence of Broadcast programming:

(1) The freedom and independence of broadcast programming shall be guaranteed.
(2) No one shall regulate or interfere with the broadcast programming unless as prescribed by this Act or other acts.
(3) A broadcasting business operator shall appoint a person in charge of broadcast programming, and make an official announcement of his name during broadcasting hours at least once in a day, and guarantee the autonomous broadcast programming for the person in charge of broadcast programming.
(4) A broadcasting business operator engaged in general programming or specialized programming of news reports shall, in order to guarantee an autonomy in the production of broadcast programs, institute a covenant on broadcast programming, reflecting the options of the persons engaged in data collection and production, and shall publicly announce it.[147]

172. Yet the issue of political independence of broadcasters has been debated for a long time even until now.

§2. Fair Representation in Election Periods

173. In Article 82(1) of the Public Official Election Act, when a broadcasting business operator holds a dialogue and discussion meeting and wants to broadcast it, it should be broadcasted unedited.[148] As a general rule, broadcasting companies are obliged to comply with public interest, diversity, and truth in organizing broadcasting program.[149] Article 8 of the Public Official Election Act also reads:

> Where a person who manages and controls broadcasting, a newspaper, wire service, magazine or other publications, a person who edits, gathers data, writes or reports, or any Internet press agency provided for in the provisions of Article 8-5(1) reports or comments on the platform or policy of a political party, political views or other matters of a candidate (including a person who intends to be a candidate; hereafter the same shall apply in this Article) and broadcasts or reports the interview or discussion in which a representative of a political party, a candidate or his/her proxy participates, he/she or it shall be fair.[150]

147. Broadcasting Act, Art. 4.
148. Public Official Election Act, Art. 82(1).
149. Broadcasting Act, Art. 69(1).
150. Public Official Election Act, Art. 8.

§3. News and Current Affairs Programs

174. According to Article 69 of the Broadcasting Act, a broadcasting business operator that engages in general programming should include broadcast programs related to news reports, culture and entertainment.[151] When organizing broadcasting programs, decision-makers must present in a balanced manner various subject matters, such as politics, economy, society and culture.[152] Article 50 of the Enforcement Decree of the Broadcasting Act includes specific standards with respect to each category.

§4. Political Advertising

175. Political advertising has a great impact on democratic electoral processes. Political advertising accounts for a larger portion of the contemporary election campaigns due to changes in the election environment, such as increased influence of the media and decreased influence of large-scale mass meetings such as party speeches. In South Korea, political advertising on television was allowed for the first time in 1992.[153]

176. According to the Public Official Election Act, political advertising on television is only applied to elections for the president, proportional representatives at the National Assembly, and provincial governors.[154] Broadcasting time for a political advertising cannot exceed one minute at a time.[155]

151. Broadcasting Act, Art. 69.
152. *Ibid.*, Art. 69(2).
153. Jinyoung Tak, Lynda Lee Kaid & Soobum Lee, *A Cross-Cultural Study of Political Advertising in the United States and Korea*, 24 Communication Research 413, 421 (1997).
154. Article 70(1) of Public Official Election Act states: "A candidate (referring to the political party that recommends its candidate in the presidential election and the political party that recommends its candidates in the election of the proportional representative National Assembly members …) may run an advertisement of the platform or policy of the political party to which he/she belongs, his/her political views, and other matters necessary for publicity using television or radio broadcasting facilities … during the election campaign period, pursuant to the following, but the advertising time shall not exceed one minute at a time. In such cases, the re-broadcasting shall be included in the calculation of the advertisement frequency, but a concurrent use of the relevant broadcasting networks with a selection of one television or radio broadcasting facility shall be deemed one time: 1. Presidential election: Up to 30 times for television and radio broadcasts, respectively; 2. Election of proportional representative National Assembly members: Up to 15 times for television and radio broadcasts, respectively; 3. Election of Mayor/*Do* Governor: Up to five times for television and radio broadcasts by using local broadcasting facilities, respectively."
155. Public Official Election Act, Art. 70(1).

Chapter 5. Advertising Rules

§1. Various Forms of Commercial Communications

177. A broadcasting business operator is expected to make a distinction between broadcasting programs and commercials.[156] According to Article 73 of the Broadcasting Act, categories of commercials include:

(1) Broadcasting program commercials: Commercials programmed to be aired before and after broadcasting programs (referring to the time from the announcement of the sign-on title to the beginning of main broadcasting programs and from the ending of main broadcasting programs to the announcement of the sign-off title).
(2) Commercial breaks: Commercials programmed to be aired during the time one broadcasting program is interrupted between the beginning of such broadcasting program and the ending of such broadcasting program.
(3) Spot commercials: Commercials programmed to be aired between one broadcasting program and another broadcasting program.
(4) Commercial captions: Commercials aired in the form of letters or pictures regardless of broadcasting programs.
(5) Time signal commercials: Commercials aired when the present time is announced.
(6) Virtual commercials: Commercials that insert virtual images created using computer graphics in broadcast programs.
(7) Product placements: Commercials that expose products, trademarks, names or logos of companies or services and others within broadcast programs.[157]

178. It is important to note that commercial breaks (referring to commercials that are programmed to be aired during the time when one broadcasting program is interrupted between the beginning and the ending of such broadcasting program) were not permitted until recently for terrestrial broadcasters with a few exceptions such as sports games, cultural or art events.[158] In South Korea, starting June 2021, terrestrial broadcasters can air commercial breaks.[159]

179. In 2008, the Constitutional Court of Korea ruled that allowing Korea Broadcast Advertising Corporation and its affiliates a monopoly over advertising

156. According to Art. 59(1) of the Enforcement Decree of the Broadcasting Act, "a broadcasting business operator shall continue displaying the caption 'commercial' of a size at least 1/64 of the screen to be clearly distinguishable from the screen on the upper left or upper right corner of the screen while airing commercials for a broadcast program mainly viewed by children (referring to broadcast content which help children grow healthily, develop their emotion, and establish cultural diversity, targeting children under the age of 13 …) and sport commercial messages before and after such broadcast program."
157. Broadcasting Act, Art. 73.
158. *See* http://www.koreaherald.com/view.php?ud=20210114001090.
159. *Ibid.*

sales on terrestrial television and radio stations was unconstitutional because it violated freedom of occupation of private advertising agencies.[160] Since the ruling, the Act on Broadcast Advertising Sales Agencies, etc. was enacted. The purpose of that Act is "to promote competition in the market for broadcast advertising sales, establish order in fair trade, and thus contribute to vitalizing the market for broadcast advertising and realizing the public good and public interests as well as variety in broadcasting services by providing matters regarding broadcast advertising, including sales agency services for broadcast advertising, and matters necessary for the incorporation of the Korea Broadcast Advertising Corporation."[161]

§2. Restrictions on Content

180. In 2008, the Constitutional Court of South Korea held that subjecting broadcast advertisements to prior review is not allowed given that it constitutes unconstitutional prior censorship prohibited by the Constitution.[162]

181. As a general rule, under Article 33 of the Broadcasting Act, the Korea Communications Standards Commission (KCSC) plays a major role in the review of broadcasters to promote public interest and fairness.[163] According to Article 33(2), review regulations cover issues related to maintaining the fundamental democratic order, veneration of human rights, public morals and social ethics, gender equality, and protecting sound family lives.[164] Regulations concerning Deliberation on Broadcasting Advertising have articles on general standards (Articles 3–24), regulations by item (Articles 25–40), and prohibitions and limitations (Articles 41–44).

182. In addition, the Broadcasting Act has a provision about self-review. Article 86 of the Broadcasting Act reads:

(1) A broadcasting business operator shall establish an organization to review broadcast programs in (excluding broadcast programs concerning news reports) before they are broadcasted. A community radio broadcasting business operator shall hold broadcasting review meetings in which the audience living within the coverage area participate, at least once a year.
(2) No broadcasting business operator shall broadcast any commercial that contains any content misleading viewers, including falsity and exaggeration.

160. Constitutional Court, decided on November 27, 2008, 2006HunMa352.
161. Act on Broadcast Advertising Sales Agencies, Etc., Art. 1.
162. Constitutional Court, decided on June 26, 2008, 2005HunMa506.
163. Broadcasting Act, Art. 33.
164. *Ibid.*, Art. 33(2).

(3) A broadcasting business operator may review commercials internally before broadcasting them, or by entrusting a broadcast-related institution or agency reported to the Korea Communications Commission to conduct review.[165]

§3. TIME AND FREQUENCY RESTRICTIONS

183. In 2015, the KCC adopted "advertising regulations for total amount."[166] The underlying rationale for this change was to help broadcast business operators freely organize advertisements in consideration of ad rate and audience rating within the allotted time. The advertising regulations for total amount refer to a system in which the government only regulates the total amount of commercials instead of regulating time and frequency of aired commercials for each type of commercial. Under the Broadcasting Act, for example, a broadcast business operator decides the time and frequency of commercials for each type of commercial.[167] These regulations are not content-regulations but content-neutral regulations.

§4. SPONSORSHIP

184. In the Broadcasting Act, sponsorship notice is defined as providing the expenses, goods, services, manpower, or place needed directly or indirectly for the production of a broadcast program by another person and notifying the name of sponsor.[168] Sponsorship can be concentrated on popular programs and is potentially subject to the influence of those who want to be a sponsor, which leads to the necessity of appropriate regulation. Sponsorship notice should be clearly distinguished from the broadcast program and commercials.

185. In 2016, the KCC revised the rules regarding sponsorship notice. To increase transparency of management of sponsorship among broadcasting business operators, the KCC also proposed guidelines on sponsoring notification:

1. Broadcasting business operators shall not receive sponsorship for programs on current affairs and reporting, commentation or current affairs debate which are banned for sponsorship notification. However, sponsorship of venue, clothes, props, and information which are inevitably necessary for the program are allowed.
2. Broadcasting business operators shall not receive sponsorship from political parties or organizations representing political interest or those who produce or sell goods or services which are prohibited from being advertised in broadcasting.

---

165. *Ibid.*, Art. 86.
166. *See* https://www.yna.co.kr/view/AKR20150421161900033.
167. Broadcasting Act, Art. 73.
168. *Ibid.*, Art. 2.

3. Broadcasting business operators shall not produce or plan programs which may bring sponsor's commercial impact.
4. Broadcasting business operators shall not use expressions which may recommend purchase of goods or services of sponsors or a 3rd party when producing broadcasting programs.
5. Broadcasting business operators shall offer educational programs for employees to be familiar with relevant laws necessary to raise transparency in sponsorship operation.[169]

§5. PRODUCT PLACEMENT

186. It can be difficult for viewers to distinguish product placements that expose products, trademarks, names or logos of companies or services and others within broadcast programs from broadcast programs.[170] It is even difficult to make a distinction between sponsorship and product placement. A broadcasting business operator can sell product placements through a media lab and later pays the Broadcasting Communications Development Fund which was established to support the development of broadcasting communications in South Korea. The Broadcasting Act includes a provision that concerns product placements. Thus, an external producer that produces a broadcast program can sell a product placement.[171] Article 73(6) of the Broadcasting Act states:

> A broadcasting business operator and an external producer shall agree upon whether a product placement under paragraph (5) violates any provision of paragraph (2), the Review Regulations formulated under Article 33(1), and the self-review standards formulated under Article 86, following procedures prescribed by Presidential Decree, before outsourcing the sales of, or entering into an agreement for the sales of, the product placement.[172]

---

169. Korea Communications Commission, Annual Report 49 (2016).
170. According to the Enforcement Decree of the Broadcasting Act, product placements need to abide by the following standards: "1. The size of product placements (referring to the size of the mark of a product, such as the label or log, exposed by product placement) shall not exceed ¼ of the screen: Provided, That it shall not exceed 1/3 of the screen in cases of mobile multimedia programs; 2. Where a broadcast program contains any product placement, a caption indicating that this program contains the product placement shall be displayed before the broadcast program starts, to make viewers clearly aware thereof; 3. No product placement shall affect the content or format of the relevant broadcast program; 4; The products, etc. featured by product placement shall not be mentioned nor the purchase and use of such products, etc. shall not be recommended in the relevant broadcast program; 5. No product placement shall interrupt the flow of viewers' watching."
171. Broadcasting Act, Art. 73(5).
172. *Ibid.*, Art. 73(6).

Chapter 6. Right to Information

§1. Access to Major Events

187. The Broadcasting Act defines "general watching and listening right" as "the right of the people to watch and listen to the broadcasts of sports games and other major events that are greatly popular with them."[173] This is to better protect people's access to major events. Ensuring access to major events, such as sporting events, is important especially when numerous programs are available and audiences are fragmented. These events can enable people to have a shared viewing experience at the national level. Article 76(2) of the Broadcasting Act states:

> The Korea Communications Commission shall publish the sports games and other major events that are greatly popular with the people ... after going through the deliberation thereon by the General Viewing and Listening Right Guarantee Committee provided for in Article 76-2. In such cases, the Korea Communications Commission shall consider the opinions of the Minister of Culture, Sports and Tourism, broadcasting business operators and viewers and listeners.[174]

§2. Short News Reporting

188. In the Broadcasting Act, a news report is defined as "programming a broadcast program of coverage and report, reviews, commentaries, etc."[175] There is no specific provision in the Broadcasting Act. Article 69 of the Broadcasting Act requires a broadcasting business operator to include news reports in compliance with the standards imposed by Presidential Decree. It is important to note that current news reporting that consists of simple facts is not protected under the Copyright Act.[176]

173. *Ibid.*, Art. 2.
174. *Ibid.*, Art. 76(2).
175. *Ibid.*, Art. 2.
176. Copyright Act, Art. 7(5).

Chapter 7. Access to Networks

§1. MUST CARRY RULES

189. According to Article 78 of the Broadcasting Act, cable television broadcasting operators and satellite broadcasting operators (except satellite DBM), and cable television relay broadcasting operators must carry, simultaneously, two public broadcasting channels, KBS1 TV and EBS TV, without modifications.[177] There are two types of retransmission according to Article 61 of the Enforcement Decree of the Broadcasting Act: (1) simultaneous retransmission which refers to the simultaneous retransmission of broadcasting programs without modifications and (2) time-delayed retransmission which refers to the retransmission of recorded programs at different times without modifications.[178]

§2. OTHER ACCESS OBLIGATIONS FOR NETWORKS

190. A broadcasting business operator is expected to make its broadcast programs available to other broadcasting business operators at fair and reasonable market prices and without any discrimination.[179] When a foreign broadcasting business operator intends to retransmit their programs in South Korea through other broadcasting business operators, the person should obtain approval from the Minister of Science, ICT and Future Planning. Specific guidelines are presented in Article 61-3 of Enforcement Decree of the Broadcasting Act. In addition, Article 52 of the Enforcement Decree of the Broadcasting Act requires broadcast business operators to enable support for viewing by persons with disabilities.[180]

177. Broadcasting Act, Art. 78.
178. *See* https://elaw.klri.re.kr/kor_service/lawView.do?hseq=50339&lang=ENG.
179. Broadcasting Act, Art. 76(1).
180. Article 52(1) of the Enforcement Decree of the Broadcasting Act states: "In order to support viewing by persons with disabilities pursuant to Article 69(9) of the Act, a broadcasting business operator shall use sign languages, closed caption subtitles, screen commentaries, etc. for broadcast programs ... : Provided, That the Korea Communications Commission may determine and announce the mandatory ratio of broadcasting for persons with disabilities in the case of broadcast programs, other than the following broadcast programs, considering the production conditions of the relevant broadcasting business operator and the audience's demand."

Chapter 8. Standards and Interoperability

191. The Broadcasting Act stipulates matters necessary for the proper operation of the broadcasting business. Given the importance of enabling the broadcasting technology infrastructure to properly operate, broadcasting business operators are required to meet certain technological standards and facilities.[181] In addition, broadcasting programs should be distributed in a timely manner and broadcast content should be managed after deliberation even after the end of the broadcast period. Hence, the Broadcasting Act stipulates provisions concerning production, distribution, and preservation of broadcast programs.

192. On the other hand, according to Article 97 of the Broadcasting Act, the government or the KCC may support projects that promote international cooperation such as international exchange with foreign broadcasting institutions, co-production of broadcasting programs, mutual exchange of personnel, and co-development of broadcasting-related technologies.[182]

---

181. For example, Art. 79 of the Broadcasting Act regulates technological standards and completion inspection, etc. concerning CATV broadcasting station facilities.
182. Broadcasting Act, Art. 97.

Part IV. Ownership Regulation

193. Traditionally and in other countries, ownership regulation is designed to ensure diversity and done through regulations in broadcasting. Korea also has ownership regulation aiming at diversity in broadcasting, but Korea has some ownership regulation rules in newspaper. Chapter 1 discusses something called "mono medium ownership regulation." This type of ownership regulation is concerning one person/company owning one newspaper or one broadcasting station. Chapter 1 will also examine how media ownership regulation in general is being enforced in Korea.

194. The second type of ownership regulation concerns rules on owning multiple media businesses in the same kind of media (i.e., a person or corporation owning multiple number of broadcasting stations within the same type of broadcasting business). This is called "multiple media ownership regulation" and there is no multiple media ownership regulation in newspapers in Korea.

195. Chapter 3 discusses "cross-media ownership regulation" that regulates ownership in different kinds of media (i.e., a person or corporation owning multiple media business that include broadcast and cable television, newspaper, and various other entities).

Chapter 1. Mono Medium Ownership Regulation and Enforcement Tools in Ownership Regulation in General

§1. Newspapers

196. Under the Act on the Promotion of Newspapers, Etc., a person who intends to publish a newspaper or to electronically publish an online newspaper or online news service is required to register with the government. And, those who are disqualified as a publisher under this Act include any entity in which any foreigner holds shares or equities in excess of the rate falling under any of the following: 30/100 in cases of a daily newspaper; 50/100 in cases of a newspaper, other than a daily newspaper.[183]

197. Article 18 of this Act imposes restrictions on ownership of general daily newspapers by large enterprises. Specifically, it states:

(1) A company belonging to a conglomerate (hereinafter referred to as "large enterprise") falling under the standards prescribed by Presidential Decree, such as total asset, etc. from among the conglomerates under subparagraph 2 of Article 2 of the Monopoly Regulation and Fair Trade Act and companies affiliated therewith (including those in a special relationship prescribed by Presidential Decree) shall not acquire or own in excess of one-half of the stocks issued by a juristic person operating a general daily newspaper or in excess of one-half of the equities thereof.[184]
(2) The number of persons in kinship under Article 777 of the Civil Act from among the directors (referring to executive officers in cases of an unlimited partnership and to partners with unlimited liability in cases of a limited partnership company) of a juristic person operating a general daily newspaper shall not exceed one-third of the total number of directors.[185]

198. There are mainly three measures to be taken in time of violation of ownership restriction imposed by Article 18. First, no one who has acquired or owns stocks or equities in violation of Article 18 shall exercise voting rights in such excess portion.[186] Second, the mayors or *Do* Governors shall order those who have acquired or owned stocks or equities, in violation of Article 18 to correct such violation within a specified period of not more than six months.[187] Third, any person who possesses stocks or equities in violation of Article 18 shall be subject to an administrative fine not exceeding KRW 20 million.[188]

183. Act on the Promotion of Newspapers, Etc., Art. 13(4)3.
184. *Ibid.*, Art. 18(1).
185. *Ibid.*, Art. 18(2).
186. *Ibid.*, Art. 19(1).
187. *Ibid.*, Art. 19(2).
188. *Ibid.*, Art. 39(1)10.

§2. BROADCASTING

199. When a broadcasting entity issues stocks, they shall be registered ones.[189] Article 8 of the Broadcasting Act contains various provisions concerning ownership restrictions. Some of the provisions can be categorized as regulations on mono medium ownership. First, no one shall own more than 40/100 of the total stocks or equity shares of a terrestrial broadcasting business entity or a program provider that engages in general programming or specialized programming of news reports, including the stocks or equity shares owned by persons having a special relationship prescribed by Presidential Decree (hereinafter referred to as "related party").[190] This provision has certain exceptions for ownership by the State or a local government, by the FBC, and by a broadcasting entity that aims at missionary work of religion.[191] The ratio had increased from 30/100 to 40/100 in July 2009.

200. Second, a company belonging to an enterprise group that meets the criteria prescribed by Presidential Decree, including the gross amount of assets, among the enterprise groups defined under subparagraph 2 of Article 2 of the Monopoly Regulation and Fair Trade Act (hereinafter referred to as "conglomerate"), and its affiliates (including related parties) shall not own more than 10/100 of the total stocks or equity shares of a terrestrial broadcasting business entity, and shall not own 30/100 of the total stocks or equity shares of a program provider engaging in general programming or specialized programming of new reports.[192] This change also happened in July 2009.

201. Third, no political party is allowed to own any stocks or equity shares of a broadcasting business entity.[193] Fourth, the following entities are not allowed to become a community radio broadcasting business entity: the Government of the Republic of Korea, a local government, a religious organization, a political party, and a person who intends to operate a community radio broadcasting business for profit.[194]

202. Article 14 of the Broadcasting Act contains various provisions concerning foreign capital investment and contribution. These provisions set different maximum ratio of foreign capital investment to the total stocks or equity for various types of broadcasting entity.

203. First, no terrestrial broadcasting business entity or community radio broadcasting business entity shall receive an investment or a contribution of property from a foreign government or organization, a foreigner, and a corporation, stocks or equity shares of which are owned by a foreign government or organization or a foreigner in excess of the ratio prescribed by Presidential Decree (hereinafter referred

189. Broadcasting Act, Art. 8(1).
190. *Ibid.*, Art. 8(2).
191. *Ibid.*
192. *Ibid.*, Art. 8(3).
193. *Ibid.*, Art. 8(10).
194. *Ibid.*, Art. 8(14).

to as "foreigners, etc.").[195] This prohibition does not apply to cases in which terrestrial broadcasters or community radio stations receive property contributions from a foreign organization operated for facilitating education, athletics, religion, charity and other international friendship, if approval from the KCC has been obtained.

204. Second, a program provider engaging in general programming or a CATV relay broadcasting business entity shall not receive an investment or contribution of property from foreigners, etc. in excess of 20/100 of the total stocks or equity shares of the relevant corporation.[196] Third, a program provider engaging in specialized programming of news reports shall not receive an investment or contribution of property from foreigners, etc. in excess of 10/100 of the total stocks or equity shares of the relevant corporation.[197] Fourth, a CATV broadcasting business entity, satellite broadcasting business entity and program provider (excluding a person engaging in general programming or specialized programming of news reports) or a signal transmission network business entity shall not receive an investment or contribution of property from foreigners, etc. in excess of 49/100 of the total stocks or equity shares of the relevant corporation.[198] But, in cases of program providers (excluding a person engaging in general programming, specialized programming of news reports, or specialized programming featuring and marketing products), a foreign corporation is not considered "foreigners, etc." if the corporation belongs to a foreign country that has bilateral or multi-lateral free trade agreements with Korea.[199]

205. There are mainly four measures to be taken in time of violation of ownership restriction imposed by Article 8 of the Broadcasting Act or Article 14 of the Act. First, no person who owns stocks or equity shares, in violation of Article 8, shall exercise his/her voting right to the stocks or equity shares owned in excess.[200] Second, the Minister of Science, ICT and Future Planning or the KCC may order a person who violates Article 8 to rectify the relevant violation within a given period not exceeding six months.[201] This is called "a corrective order." Third, a person who violates a corrective order issued under Article 8(13) or under Article 14(6) is subject to imprisonment for not more than one year or a fine not exceeding KRW thirty million.[202] Fourth, in violation of Article 8 or Article 14, the Minister of Science, ICT and Future Planning or the KCC may issue an order revoking a license, approval or registration, fully or partially suspending the relevant business, suspending advertisement, or reducing the period of validity of a license and approval granted under Article 16 of the Broadcasting Act within a specified period not exceeding six months.[203]

---

195. *Ibid.*, Art. 14(1).
196. *Ibid.*, Art. 14(2).
197. *Ibid.*
198. *Ibid.*, Art. 14(3).
199. *Ibid.*
200. *Ibid.*, Art. 8(12).
201. *Ibid.*, Art. 8(13).
202. *Ibid.*, Art. 106(1)2 & Art. 106(1)3.
203. *Ibid.*, Art. 18(1)2 & Art. 18(1)4.

Chapter 2. Multiple Media Ownership Regulation

§1. Broadcasting

206. There is regulation regarding owning multiple broadcasting companies within the same type of broadcasting while there is no such regulation in newspapers. First, Article 8(8) of the Broadcasting Act states that "a terrestrial broadcasting business entity, a CATV broadcasting business entity, or a satellite broadcasting business entity shall not concurrently operate another terrestrial broadcasting business, CATV broadcasting business, or satellite broadcasting business respectively, or own their stocks or equity shares in excess of limits prescribed by Presidential Decree,[204] in consideration of market shares, the number of business entities, etc."[205]

207. Similarly, Article 8(9) of this Act prohibits a program provider from concurrently operating another program provider or owning its stocks or equity shares in excess of limits prescribed by Presidential Decree,[206] in consideration of market share, the number of business entities, etc.[207] Lastly, Article 8(15) of this Act stipulates that no community radio broadcasting business entity shall own more than one broadcasting station.[208]

204. For the specific regulations, *see* Art. 4(7) of the Enforcement Decree of the Broadcasting Act.
205. Broadcasting Act, Art. 8(8).
206. For the specific regulations, *see* Art. 4(8) of the Enforcement Decree of the Broadcasting Act.
207. Broadcasting Act, Art. 8(9).
208. *Ibid.*, Art. 8(15).

Chapter 3. Cross-Media Ownership Regulation

208. Cross-media ownership regulation is imposed on cases in which one entity tries to own multiple kinds of media – for example, a newspaper company owning a broadcasting station. Paragraph (3) through paragraph (7) of Article 8 of the Broadcasting Act are related to cross-media ownership. Also, paragraph (16) and paragraph (17) of Article 8 of the Broadcasting Act concern cross-media ownership.

209. First, a corporation (including related parties) that publishes daily newspapers under the Act on the Promotion of Newspapers, Etc. (hereinafter referred to as "daily newspaper") or runs news communications under the Act on Promotion of News Communications (hereinafter referred to as "news communications") shall not own more than 10/100 of the total stocks or equity shares of a terrestrial broadcasting business entity, and shall not own 30/100 of the total stocks or equity shares of a program provider engaging in general programming or specialized programming of new reports.[209] Relatedly, a corporation (including related parties) that publishes a daily newspaper or runs news communications shall not own more than 49/100 of the total stocks or equity shares of any CATV broadcasting business entity or satellite broadcasting business entity.[210] In addition, a corporation (including related parties) that runs a daily newspaper of which subscription rate is 20/100 or higher shall not concurrently run terrestrial broadcasting business and program-providing business that engages in general programming or specialized programming of news reports.[211]

210. Second, a terrestrial broadcasting business entity, a CATV broadcasting business entity, and a satellite broadcasting business entity shall not mutually and concurrently operate their business or own their stocks or equity shares in excess of limits prescribed by Presidential Decree,[212] in consideration of market shares, the number of business entities, etc.[213] Relatedly, a terrestrial broadcasting business entity, a CATV broadcasting business entity, a satellite broadcasting business entity, a program provider and a signal transmission network business entity shall not mutually and concurrently operate their business or own their stocks or equity

209. *Ibid.*, Art. 8(3).
210. *Ibid.*, Art. 8(5).
211. *Ibid.*, Art. 8(4).
212. As amended on Jan. 26, 2010, the ratio is 33%. *See* Art. 4(5) of the Enforcement Decree of the Broadcasting Act.
213. Broadcasting Act, Art. 8(6).

shares in excess of limits prescribed by Presidential Decree,[214] in consideration of market shares, broadcasting fields, the number of business entities, etc.[215]

211. Third, no CATV broadcasting business entity shall provide a service in excess of one-third of the total number of subscribers to pay television service, including CATV broadcasting, satellite broadcasting and Internet multimedia broadcasting.[216] Relatedly, no satellite broadcasting business entity shall provide a service in excess of one-third of the total number of subscribers to pay television service, including CATV broadcasting, satellite broadcasting, and Internet multimedia broadcasting.[217]

214. As amended on Jan. 26, 2010, the limits are as follows: "1. a specific terrestrial broadcasting business entity runs a program providing business in excess of 3/100 (if the number calculated by multiplying the total number of business entities by 3/100 is less than six, it shall be six) of the total number of business entities by a TV programming provider, radio programming provider, or data programming provider (referring to where he/she concurrently runs any other business or owns at least 5/100 of the total stocks or equity shares thereof; 2. Where a specific cable television broadcasting business entity or satellite broadcasting business entity runs a program providing business in excess of 1/5 of the total number of business entities by a TV programming provider, radio programming provider, or data programming provider." *See* Art. 4(6) of the Enforcement Decree of the Broadcasting Act.

215. Broadcasting Act, Art. 8(7).

216. *Ibid.*, Art. 8(16).

217. *Ibid.*, Art. 8(17).

Part V. Supervision: Media Regulator

Chapter 1. Organization

212. South Korea has a central administrative agency, the KCC, responsible for regulating broadcasting and telecommunications. KCC's sister agency, the KCSC has the authority to deliberate on the broadcast content and online content. KCSC aims to ensure the public responsibility and fairness of broadcast content and to provide an online environment in which safe and useful information is available. Meanwhile, the PAC is a quasi-judicial entity that settles disputes arising from any news reports by print media, electronic media, and Internet newspapers.[218]

§1. Korea Communications Commission

213. KCC was formed in 2008 under the Act on the Establishment of and Operation of KCC[219] in order to (1) enhance the freedom, public nature and public interest of broadcasting by actively responding to the convergence of broadcasting and communications, and (2) contribute to the protection of rights and interests of the public and the improvement of the public welfare.[220] KCC is a central administrative agency under the control of the President. KCC is responsible for regulating the broadcasting and telecommunications and for protecting users.[221]

214. The KCC consists of five standing commissioners, including a Chairperson and a Vice Chairperson. The commissioners are appointed by the President, and the Chairperson goes through confirmation hearing processes of the National Assembly.[222] Among the five commissioners, two are nominated by the President, one is nominated by a political party to which the President belongs or belonged, and two are nominated by other political parties of the National Assembly. The term of office of the commissioners is three years, and consecutive appointment is permitted only once.[223] No commissioner shall be involved in political activities.[224]

218. Act on Press Arbitration and Remedies, Etc. for Damage Caused by Press Reports, Art. 7.
219. Act No. 13580.
220. Act on the Establishment of and Operation of Korea Communications Commission, Art. 1.
221. *Ibid.*, Art. 3.
222. *Ibid.*, Art. 5.
223. *Ibid.*, Art. 7.
224. *Ibid.*, Art. 9(2).

215. Along with the five commissioners, there is an executive part of KCC that oversees the management and operations of daily matters. Within the executive part, there are a Secretary-General, four bureaus, a Director General for Planning and Coordination, and a General Affairs division. The four bureaus are Broadcasting Policy Bureau, Consumer Policy Bureau, Broadcasting Infrastructure Bureau, and Mobile Distribution Investigation Bureau.

§2. Korea Communications Standards Commission

216. Another commission, the KCSC was also established in 2008 under the Act on the Establishment of and Operation of KCC. The KCSC performs its duties independently from the KCC and aims to (1) guarantee the public nature and fairness of broadcasting content, (2) create a sound culture in the areas of information and communications, and (3) create an environment where information and communications are used in an appropriate manner.[225]

217. The KCSC consists of nine members appointed by the President. Among the nine, three members, including the Chairperson and a Vice Chairperson, are full-time standing commissioners. The term of office of the commissioners is three years, and consecutive appointment is permitted only once.[226] KCSC commissioners are called "deliberators,"[227] for KCSC deliberates on broadcasting content and online content.

218. The executive part of KCSC is made up of a Secretariat General, an Audit and Inspection Office, an Operation Support division, four bureaus, a Planning and Coordination Office, a Remedial Center of Online Infringement, and five regional offices. The four bureaus are Broadcast Review Bureau 1, Broadcast Review Bureau 2, Internet Communications Review Bureau, and Consumer Rights Protection Bureau.[228]

§3. Press Arbitration Commission

219. The PAC was established in 1981 under the Basic Press Act. The Basic Press Act was repealed in 1987, but the PAC remained. In 2005, the Act on Press Arbitration and Remedies, Etc. for Damage Caused by Press Reports (hereinafter referred to as "the Press Arbitration Act") was enacted to renew the role of PAC as "to settle disputes arising from and related to any press report or medium of the press, etc. by conciliation or arbitration as well as to deliberate on infringements caused thereby."[229]

225. *Ibid.*, Art. 18.
226. *Ibid.*
227. *Ibid.*, Art. 18(3).
228. KCSC, *Organization>Organization Chart*, https://www.kocsc.or.kr/eng/Chart.php.
229. Act on Press Arbitration and Remedies, Etc. for Damage Caused by Press Reports, Art. 7(1).

220. PAC is composed of forty to ninety arbitration commissioners, including one Chairman who represents and supervises PAC and two Vice Chairmen. The arbitration commissioners are appointed by the Minister of Culture, Sports and Tourism, from among judges in active service, lawyers, former journalists with more than ten years of experience, and distinguished persons in the press community serve as commissioners.[230]

221. PAC mainly functions through arbitral tribunals. There are eight arbitral tribunals in Seoul and ten arbitral tribunals in metropolitan and provincial cities other than Seoul. Each arbitral tribunal has five commissioners, including one chief commissioner. The PAC Chairman appoints the chief commissioner, and the chief commissioner shall be a judge in active service or a lawyer.[231]

222. The Secretariat is responsible for PAC's overall operations and is made up of three headquarters. The main tasks of the secretariat are counseling the aggrieved party, advising on methods of redemption, conducting research and publishing for the press arbitration system, promoting and educating on the Commission and the press arbitration system, and sponsoring in-house seminars and public forums.[232]

230. *Ibid.*, Art. 7(3).
231. *Ibid.*
232. Press Arbitration Commission, *Press Arbitration Commission*, 9 (2014).

Chapter 2. Tasks

§1. Korea Communications Commission

223. Article 2 of the Act on the Establishment of and Operation of KCC pronounces three principles under which KCC shall operate. The three principles are (1) to endeavor after the welfare of users of broadcasting and communications and the provision of general services; (2) to endeavor to create a fair competitive environment for broadcasting and communications business; and (3) to take necessary measures to ensure the broadcasting and communications business serves the public interests.[233]

224. Article 11 of the Act on the Establishment of and Operation of KCC stipulates four areas under the jurisdiction of KCC. They are:

(1) matters concerning policies on broadcast advertising, policies on evaluation of programming, planning for broadcasting promotion, planning for broadcasting policies, policies on terrestrial broadcasting, and policies on broadcasting channels;
(2) matters concerning the overall control of research and planning, market surveys on broadcasting and communications, protection of users of broadcasting and communications, promotion of viewers' rights and interests, and ethics relating to protecting personal information;
(3) matters concerning the management of frequencies used for broadcasting services; and
(4) other matters determined as duties of the Commission by this Act or other acts.[234]

225. Article 12 of the Act on the Establishment of and Operation of KCC lists twenty-nine matters subject to deliberation and resolution of KCC. The twenty-nine matters are:

(1) matters concerning basic plans on broadcasting and those on the regulation of communications;
(2) matters concerning the recommendation on directors and the appointment of auditors for the KBS;
(3) matters concerning the appointment of directors and auditors for the FBC;
(4) matters concerning the appointment of chief executive officer, directors, and auditors for the EBS;
(5) matters concerning the research on and assessment of media diversity;
(6) matters concerning the permission and renewal of permission granted to terrestrial broadcasting business entities and community radio broadcasting business entities;

---

233. Act on the Establishment of and Operation of Korea Communications Commission, Art. 2.
234. *Ibid.*, Art. 11(1).

(7) matters concerning the approval for program-providing business entities using broadcasting channels for general programming or programming specialized in news reports;
(8) matters concerning the permission, renewal of permission, and permission for change granted to satellite broadcasting business entities, CATV broadcasting business entities, and CATV relay broadcasting business entities, as well as those concerning the consent to the enactment, modification, and repeal of related statutes;
(9) matters concerning the permission, revocation, and approval for broadcast advertising sales agencies pursuant to the Act on Broadcast Advertising Sales Agencies, Etc.;
(10) matters concerning investigation and restriction on prohibited acts by broadcasting business entities;
(11) matters concerning the investigation into and restriction on prohibited acts by broadcast advertising sales agencies;
(12) matters concerning the investigation into and restriction on prohibited acts by telecommunications business entities;
(13) matters concerning the mediation of disputes between and among broadcasting business entities and telecommunications business entities, or disputes between business entities and users, etc.;
(14) matters concerning the mediation of disputes between and among broadcast advertising sales agencies, etc.;
(15) matters concerning the response to complaints from viewers as well as the protection of users of broadcasting and communications;
(16) matters concerning the management of Community Media Foundation;
(17) matters concerning the guarantee of the universal watching and listening right;
(18) matters concerning the composition and management of the Broadcasting Evaluation Committee;
(19) matters concerning the restrictions, etc. on the share of audience of broadcasting business entities;
(20) matters concerning the disciplinary measures pursuant to the deliberation and resolution by the KCSC;
(21) matters concerning the composition and management of the Regional Broadcasting Development Committee;
(22) matters concerning the research and support with respect to the regulation of broadcasting and communications;
(23) matters concerning the international cooperation with respect to the regulation of broadcasting and communications;
(24) matters concerning the management of frequencies used for broadcasting services;
(25) matters concerning the operation, organization, and sales of broadcast programs and broadcast advertising;
(26) matters concerning the raising, management, and operation of funds related to broadcasting and communications;
(27) matters concerning the enactment, modification, and repeal of statutes concerned as well as regulations of the Commission;

(28) matters concerning the budget and budget planning of the Commission; and
(29) matters on which the Commission has deliberated and resolved pursuant to this Act or other acts.[235]

226. Article 31 paragraph (1) of the Broadcasting Act stipulates that KCC "may comprehensively evaluate the content, programming, operation, etc. of broadcast programs of a broadcasting business entity."[236] Article 31 also says that KCC may establish a Broadcast Review Committee to efficiently perform the review duties under paragraph (1).[237] While the Broadcasting Act gave KCC the authority to comprehensively evaluate the content of broadcast programs, the Act also stipulates that KCSC shall deliberate on the content of broadcast programs. The details of KCSC's duty to deliberate are discussed in the subsequent section.

§2. Korea Communications Standards Commission

227. Article 21 of the Act on the Establishment of and Operation of KCC lists eight duties of KCSC. They are:

(1) deliberation on matters falling under Article 32 of the Broadcasting Act;
(2) deliberation and resolution on sanctions, etc. under Article 100 of the Broadcasting Act;
(3) deliberation on matters falling under Article 44-7 of the Act on Promotion of Information and Communications Network Utilization and Information Protection, Etc.;
(4) deliberation on information prescribed by Presidential Decree as necessary for nurturing sound communications ethics, from among information disclosed to the public and distributed via telecommunication circuits, or requests for correction;
(5) matters concerning the soundness of information distributed via telecommunication circuits;
(6) matters concerning business plans, budget and the settlement of accounts of the Korea Communications Standards Commission;
(7) matters concerning the enactment, modification and repeal of regulations of the Korea Communications Standards Commission; and
(8) matters determined to be subject to the deliberation of the Korea Communications Standards Commission by other statutes.[238]

228. Article 32 of the Broadcasting Act requires KCSC to "deliberate and pass a resolution as to whether the content of a broadcast, a CATV relay broadcast and an electric sign board broadcast, or the content of information similar to a broadcast and the information prescribed by Presidential Decree, from among the information

235. *Ibid.*, Art. 12.
236. Broadcasting Act, Art. 31(1).
237. *Ibid.*, Art. 31(2).
238. Act on the Establishment of and Operation of Korea Communications Commission, Art. 21.

circulated through telecommunication circuits aiming at opening to the public, maintain their impartiality and public nature, and as to whether they observe public responsibilities, after they are broadcasted or circulated. In such cases, the characteristics by medium and by channel shall be taken into consideration."[239]

229. To perform this role, KCSC is asked to "formulate and publicly announce rules concerning the review of broadcasts (hereinafter referred to as 'Review Regulations')."[240] Review Regulations shall deal with the following sixteen matters:

> concerning (1) maintaining the fundamental democratic order provided in the Constitution; (2) protecting sound family lives; (3) protecting children and juveniles and sound character building; (4) public morals and social ethics; (5) gender equality; (6) advancing international friendship; (7) enhancing the rights and the interests of classes alienated by the broadcasting, such as persons with disabilities; (8) prohibition against discrimination on grounds of race, nationality, region, religion, etc.; (9) promoting national culture and cultivating national identity; (10) the impartiality and public nature of news reports or commentaries; (11) purifying a language; (12) protecting the natural environment; (13) sound consumption and protection of the rights and interests of viewers; (14) items or content prohibited from commercials under Acts and subordinate statutes; (15) the impartiality and public interest of commercials; and (16) other matters concerning the deliberation duties of the Korea Communications Standards Commission under this Act.[241]

Article 44-7 of the Information and Communications Network Act prohibits anyone from circulating unlawful information and gives KCSC the authority to deliberate on which information falls into the categories of unlawful information. The categories of unlawful information listed in Article 44-7 are:

> (1) an obscene content; (2) a content that defames other persons by divulging a fact, false fact, openly and purposely to disparage the person's reputation; (3) a content that arouses fear or apprehension by reaching other persons repeatedly in the form of code, words, sound, image, or motion pictures; (4) a content that mutilates, destroys, alters, or forges an information and communications system, data, a program, or similar or that interferes with the operation of such system, data, program, or similar without a justifiable ground; (5) a content that amounts to a media product harmful to youths under the Youth Protection Act and that is provided for profit without fulfilling the duties and obligations under relevant statutes, including the duty to verify the opposite party's age or the duty of labeling; (6) a content that falls within speculative activities prohibited by statutes; (6-2) information regarding content of transactions of personal information in violation of this Act or other statutes concerning the protection of personal information; (7) a content that

239. Broadcasting Act, Art. 32.
240. *Ibid.*, Art. 33(1).
241. *Ibid.*, Art. 33(2).

divulges a secret classified by statutes or any other State secret; (8) a content that commits an activity prohibited by the National Security Act; and (9) other information with a content that attempts, aids, or abets to commit a crime.[242]

230. In addition to asking KCSC to deliberate on unlawful information, Article 41 of the Information and Communications Network Act requires KCC to prepare a policy to protect youths from harmful information[243] circulated through information and communications networks and gives KCSC the authority to review and impose sanctions on information harmful to youths.[244]

231. KCSC receives complaints from those who are dissatisfied with or those who suffer damages from both unlawful information online and harmful information to youths online. First, the categories of unlawful information are listed in Article 44-7 of the Information and Communications Network Act as shown above. Second, harmful information to youths is information of obscenities and violence;[245] information that is deemed harmful to youths by KCSC and by the Commissions on Youth Protection. Harmful information to youths is broadly defined to mean harmful information that is "immoral, violent, obscene, speculative, and anti-social."[246]

§3. Press Arbitration Commission

232. Article 7 of the Press Arbitration Act states that PAC is established to "settle disputes arising from and related to any press report or medium of the press, etc. (hereinafter referred to as 'press reporter, etc.') by conciliation or arbitration as well as to deliberate on infringements caused thereby."[247] The term "press" is defined as "any broadcasting, newspaper, periodical including any magazine, news communications or online newspaper."[248] Article 3 of the Act guarantees the freedom and independence of the press, but Article 4 of the Act emphasizes social responsibilities of the press.

233. Furthermore, Article 5 of the Act declares that "the press, any Internet news service, or any Internet multimedia broadcasting shall not infringe on other persons' life, liberty, body, health, reputation, the secrecy and freedom pertaining to privacy, portrait, name, voice, dialogue, works, personal documents, any other personal worth, etc. (hereinafter referred to as 'personality right') and, where the press,

242. Information and Communications Network Act, Art. 44-7.
243. *Ibid.*, Art. 41(1).
244. *Ibid.*, Art. 41(2).
245. *Ibid.*, Art. 41(1).
246. *Ibid.*
247. Act on Press Arbitration and Remedies, Etc. for Damage Caused by Press Reports, Art. 7(1).
248. *Ibid.*, Art. 2(1).

etc. has infringed on any other person's personality right, such damage shall be remedied promptly in accordance with the procedure prescribed by this Act."[249] In addition to a living person, the personality rights of a deceased person are protected under Article 5-2 of this Act. PAC also receives claims from an organization, a company, and a provincial government that allegedly got damages from press reports.

234. Once a claim is received, an arbitral tribunal—composed of five or less arbitration commissioners[250]—conducts conciliation or arbitration. Both conciliation and arbitration are methods of dispute resolution involving an arbitral tribunal. In conciliation, the arbitral tribunal tries to help the involved parties reach an agreeable solution, while the tribunal's decision is binding in arbitration. Thus, for arbitration, both parties in dispute must submit a written agreement in which they commit to honor the arbitration award.

235. PAC handled approximately 3,500 conciliation and arbitration cases in 2018.[251] More than 70% of these cases were related to reports by online newspapers. The conciliation procedure is completed within two weeks, at no cost, from the point of receiving the request for conciliation. In addition to providing remedial procedures for damages, PAC also deliberates on news reports during election, provides counseling services to the aggrieved persons, and runs education programs.

249. *Ibid.*, Art. 5.
250. *Ibid.*, Art. 9.
251. Yonhap News Agency (2019.1.14), "3,562 applications for media mediation last year increased by 10.3% … Internet 70% or more," URL, https://www.yna.co.kr/view/AKR20190114143700005.

Chapter 3. Sanctioning Powers

§1. Korea Communications Commission/Korea Communications Standards Commission

236. As shown above, KCC and KCSC are sister commissions. KCC delegated the authority to review content to KCSC. KCSC formulates Review Regulations (i.e., content review guidelines) and deliberates on content. But, the sanctioning powers are exercised through KCC. Many of KCC's sanctioning powers come from the fact that KCC oversees the approval and renewal of broadcast licenses.[252]

237. When a broadcasting business entity, a CATV relay broadcasting business entity, an electric sign board broadcasting business entity, or an external producer (hereinafter referred to as "a broadcaster, etc.") violates any provision of KCSC's Review Regulations, KCC imposes a penalty of not more than KRW 50 million, or imposes sanctions under Article 100 of Broadcasting Act, considering the cause, gravity, and frequency of the violation. The same may be applied when a broadcaster, etc., violates any provision of the regulations for announcement of sponsors or when KCC's "Viewers' Rights Protection Committee"[253] asks for a sanction as a result of the settlement of viewer's complaints.

238. Sanctions under Article 100 of the Broadcasting Act are three kinds. First, a correction, rectification, or suspension of the relevant broadcast program or commercial. Second, a disciplinary action against the person in charge of broadcast programming or the person related to the relevant broadcast program or commercial. Third, a caution or warning.

239. Article 100(3) of the Broadcasting Act also stipulates that KCC may impose a penalty surcharge of not more than KRW 100 million for the following grave violations: (1) A violation of KCSC's Review Regulations in terms of lewdness, decadence, violence, etc.; and (2) a violation of KCSC's Review Regulations for such reasons as appearing on broadcasting after having taken, injected, inhaled, or drunken narcotics; and (3) a repeated violation of KCSC's Review Regulations for the same reason.

240. In addition, Article 25(1) of the Act on the Establishment of and Operation of KCC states that when it is deemed that online information violates KCSC's Review Regulations, KCC may order a provider of information and communications services or a manager or an operator of a message board to reject, suspend, or restrict the handling of illegal information under Article 44-7 of the Information and Communications Network Act.[254]

252. Broadcasting Act, Art. 9.
253. *Ibid.*, Art. 35.
254. Act on the Establishment of and Operation of Korea Communications Commission, Art. 25(1).

§2. PRESS ARBITRATION COMMISSION

241. PAC provides a form of an alternative dispute resolution, but PAC's decisions are binding decisions. Unlike other self-regulatory organizations in other countries, PAC is funded by government and its commissioners are commissioned by the Minister of Culture, Sports and Tourism.[255]

242. Under the Act on Press Arbitration and Remedies, Etc. for Damage Caused by Press Reports, the aggrieved party can apply for conciliation or arbitration within three months from the date of its awareness of the news report in question. The remedies that the aggrieved party may seek for are: (1) right to require relevant press organization, etc., to report corrected statement (i.e., a right to request correction of the original news story);[256] (2) right to require relevant press organization, etc., to report contradictory statement (i.e., a right of reply);[257] (3) right to require relevant press organization, etc., to make further report (i.e., a right to ask for a follow-up report);[258] and (4) compensation for damage.[259] If a press organization fails to follow the decided remedy after the conciliation or arbitration process, PAC may impose a fine[260] or the petitioner may bring a lawsuit against the press organization to enforce the decision.

243. Article 6 of the Act on Press Arbitration and Remedies, Etc. for Damage Caused by Press Reports requires the following types of news media to have an ombudsman in their company "to prevent and remedy autonomously any damage caused by the press": a broadcasting business operator who conducts general programming or specialized programming on reports, a newspaper business operator who publishes a general daily newspaper, or a news communications business operator.[261] Also, Article 32 of the Act gives PAC the authority to issue "Recommendations for Correction."[262] For this, PAC reviews news reports and when PAC finds press reports that infringe on national, social, or personal legal interests PAC may recommend the relevant press organization to correct such infringements.

255. Act on Press Arbitration and Remedies, Etc. for Damage Caused by Press Reports, Art. 7(3).
256. *Ibid.*, Arts 14 & 15.
257. *Ibid.*, Art. 16.
258. *Ibid.*, Art. 17.
259. *Ibid.*, Art. 30.
260. *Ibid.*, Art. 34.
261. *Ibid.*, Art. 6.
262. *Ibid.*, Art. 32.

Selected Bibliography

Ahran Park & Kyu Ho Youm. 'Judicial Communication in South Korea: Moving Toward a More Open System?'. In *Justices and Journalists: The Global Perspective*, edited by Richard Davis & David Taras. Cambridge University Press, 2017.

Jinyoung Tak, Lynda Lee Kaid & Soobum Lee. A Cross-Cultural Study of Political Advertising in the United States and Korea, Communication Research, 1997, Volume 24 Issue 4, 413-430.

Korea Communications Commission. *Annual Report*. 2016. [In Korean]

Korea Legislation Research Institute. *Introduction to Korean Law*. Springer Science & Business Media, 2012.

Kyu Ho Youm. *Press Law in South Korea*. Iowa State University Press, 1996.

Seung Sun Lee. 40 Years of Challenges and Achievements in the Korean Press Arbitration System, Journal of Media and Defamation Law, 2021, Issue 7(1). 1-65. [In Korean]

Woo-jeong Choi. Legal Issues on the Possession and Rate of Broadcasting Systems and Newspaper for Fair Competition of Media Markets, Journal of Law and Policy, 2018, Issue 24(1). 295-332. [In Korean]

Yeong-Man Jeon. *Broadcasting and Telecommunications Law Handbook*. Jinhan M&B, 2015. [In Korean]

Index

The numbers here refer to paragraph numbers.

www.ingramcontent.com/pod-product-compliance
Lightning Source LLC
Chambersburg PA
CBHW071357230926
51846CB00002B/580
9789403539843